Crossing
the
Minefield

Crossing
the
Minefield

Tactics for Overcoming Today's Toughest Management Challenges

Robert W. Barner

American Management Association

New York • Atlanta • Boston • Chicago • Kansas City • San Francisco • Washington, D.C.
Brussels • Mexico City • Tokyo • Toronto

Library of Congress Cataloging-in-Publication Data

Barner, Robert.
    Crossing the minefield : tactics for overcoming today's toughest
    management challenges / Robert W. Barner.
        p. cm.
    Includes bibliographical references and index.
    ISBN 0-8144-0241-0
    1. Industrial management. 2. Organizational behavior.
3. Corporate culture. I. Title.
HD31.B3683 1994
658.4'06—dc20   94-25592
                                                        CIP

Printing number

10 9 8 7 6 5 4 3

To
Chris, Anthony, and **Jocelyn**
May you dream your lives and live your dreams.

Contents

Acknowledgments

Writing a book is a marathon project. It can quickly become frustrating and fatiguing if you don't have friends cheering from the sidelines. Many of the following people not only cheered but sometimes were more than willing to carry me on their shoulders. I am very indebted for their help and guidance.

I'd like to thank John Adams, Dane Blumthal, Brian Chitester, Joe Dunsmore, Cindy Durning, Joe Ferrel, Terry Geraghty, Bevan Gray, Mark Johnson, Julian Kaufmann, Patrick Miller, Ed Nolan, Jane Rose, Bob Stephens, Bob Ulevich, and Jim Yager for allowing me to share with you their experiences and suggestions.

I'd like to thank AMACOM; Crown Publishers, for permission to quote from *Teaching the Elephant to Dance* by James A. Belasco; Harper Collins; Jossey-Bass; Penguin Books; Northwestern National Life Insurance Company; *Fortune; HRMagazine; Inc.; Training & Development Journal;* and *Training Magazine* for permission to reprint materials.

Mari Suarez was very helpful in conducting background research for this project, and Julie Germond assisted in the word processing. Adrienne Hickey, Kate Pferdner, and Barbara Horowitz provided welcome editorial direction from AMACOM, and I'd like to thank Irene Majuk for all the pain that I'm putting her through to push the promotion of the book. Finally, I'd like to thank my partner in work and life, Charlotte Parry, whose name by rights should be on the front of this book with my own. Her patience and advice have been priceless.

Preface

After attempting to read and apply hundreds of management books over the last few years, I have discovered that most management books fall into one of two categories. Some authors approach management from the generic platform of standard management functions to be mastered—one chapter on how to hire the best, another on how to supervise, still another on how to conduct appraisals. Others approach managerial leadership as an internal quality; they say, "Here are the qualities, principles, and characteristics displayed by good managers/leaders. These are the things you should strive to be as a manager."

We can certainly learn a lot from both kinds of books. But, what is missing and what is needed, given the tremendously disruptive and ever-changing business environment we are operating in, is a good book about how to survive and thrive as a manager during difficult times. And that's exactly what this book is about.

If I've done my homework, you should be able to walk away from this book armed with a number of good ideas for how to overcome some of the most difficult work challenges you are likely to face as a manager. This book will show you how to cross this minefield without blowing up your team or yourself.

Three things set this book apart:

1. *The subject matter is designed for our times.* I believe that leadership in tough times requires the use of unique skills and abilities—whether in developing a fast draw and accelerating your response time to change or in banishing bedlam and burnout within high-stress work environments. The subjects covered are made for today.

2. *It focuses on the "doables."* The second unique feature of this book is that it focuses on management in the trenches. It is specifically designed for first- and second-level managers. For that reason it doesn't address just-in-time inventory systems, corporate re-engineering, or ways to re-envision the workplace. I've written this book with

the assumption that you, the reader, lack the authority and control to make systemwide, top-down changes in your company. I've therefore limited my discussions to those "doable" actions that are directly within your range of control. Everything in this book is eatable; I haven't put one thing on the plate that's undigestable.

3. *It has a flexible format: skim, probe, or training tool. Take your pick.* Readers of management books generally fall into one of three categories. First, you may be a skimmer—someone who buys leadership books each year with the intention of quickly gleaning from each of them a few ideas for application. You may be a prober—one who likes to burrow into a book, testing out all available ideas, one step at a time. Finally, you may be a training manager or human resources specialist who is examining this book for possible training applications to your organization.

The good news is that this book is designed to accommodate all these styles. To make skimming easier, I've divided each "challenge" chapter into four components:

- An introduction of the *Challenge*
- *Warning symptoms* for determining the degree to which the challenge may be affecting your team's performance
- *Strategies*, with step-by-step tactics for surviving the challenge
- A *Tool Kit* containing charts, forms, exercises, and self-assessment tools designed to help you apply the tactics and strategies

This format also allows probers to focus on a single topic and carefully test new ideas before moving on.

If you are a training manager or human resources specialist, or perhaps a line manager who takes the development of your employees seriously, you may want to glance ahead and look at the *Trainer's Guide*. This section provides formats and suggestions on how to use this book to conduct training workshops. If your company is encouraging self-directed learning and employee empowerment, you will love this section, which shows you how to integrate individual self-study with several useful group exercises.

That's it in a nutshell. I've enjoyed writing this book, and I hope that you enjoy reading it. I sincerely hope that after working with this book, you will feel that your time and money were well spent. I welcome all feedback and suggestions and can easily be reached through my publisher.

R.W.B.

The Minefield

Introduction

I'm sure that I don't have to make a hard sell to convince you that it's tough to be a manager today. If you are a manager, you can see the signs all around you.

To be a manager today means having to deal with divergent and sometimes contradictory demands. On one hand, you are told you must be cautious about taking risks, especially those that might significantly affect financial performance. At the same time, you are asked to encourage greater employee empowerment. You're told that today's big push is for quality improvement but that you must accelerate production levels so that the company can survive. One day you are told that you have bottom-line responsibility for your group's performance; the next day you hear that you should consider yourself a coach and adviser to your team.

To be a manager today means attempting to establish discipline and order in your area of responsibility, while at the same time responding to large-scale changes that are profoundly affecting the roles you are asked to play in your organization.

To be a manager today means trying to perform your best within an uncertain and unstable environment. Since 1991, managers have made up a significantly large share of the corporate downsizings, and they are likely to continue to be the professional group most vulnerable to future cost-cutting programs.

If, like many managers, you are having difficulty figuring out how to cross this minefield of disruptive change, then you've come to the right place. *Crossing the Minefield* provides a comprehensive survival package for dealing with today's toughest management challenges. I've loaded it with strategies, tactics, and tools that have proved helpful to thousands of other managers in a variety of industries.

Unsure as to whether this book is what you are looking for? Check it out by taking this four-minute test.

1. [*30 seconds*] Look at the Table of Contents and see if it reflects many of the challenges that you've been attempting to deal with.
2. [*1 minute*] Walk through the organization of the book. Its subjects are divided into challenges, strategies, tactics, and tools, which makes it easier to get the information you need.
3. [*2 minutes*] Next, check out the chapter that deals with a challenge you are confronting. You'll probably find at least four useful ideas for immediate application.
4. [*30 seconds*] Finally, review the Trainer's Guide located at the back of the book to see if it might help you develop the skills of your team.

I know that no single book can hope to serve the needs and requirements of every manager, but I feel confident that if you give *Crossing the Minefield* the four-minute test, you will be pleased with the results.

Welcome to Oz

If you are like thousands of other managers, you are probably finding your job more challenging, frustrating, and confusing than ever before. Perhaps you've heard rumors that your organization's last downsizing, which left everyone demoralized, will soon be followed by another one. Or perhaps you are still trying to figure out how to meet your department's goal of improving quality by 30 percent. It could be that you are still struggling with the aftermath of your company's cost-reduction program, which has made it impossible for you to get a fifty-dollar expense voucher approved without three managerial signatures. Or you could be one of many managers who are attempting to build cooperative teamwork within an environment characterized by rapidly deteriorating group relationships.

How secure do you feel about your job? What do you think the future holds for managers? I've discussed this issue with hundreds of managers, representing a variety of organizations. Almost all of these managers, when they've had the opportunity to speak candidly, have told me that they are under more work pressure than ever before. This pressure stems not only from the increasingly stringent standards against which managerial performance is being evaulated but also from the serious risks now associated with job failure.

If you follow the major business publications, you know that the marketplace can be quite unforgiving to managers who are unable to master today's new work challenges. According to Eric Greenberg, survey director at the American Management Association, managers made up between 18 and 22 percent of terminated workers, although they make up no more than 5 to 8 percent of the workforce in downsized organizations.[1] These displaced managers tend to be older than those dismissed in earlier cutbacks; in 1984 the average age of downsized managers was forty-one, whereas by 1990 it was forty-six.[2] This age shift has increased the trauma produced by job termination, since older managers often face greater lifestyle adjustment problems and

must swim upstream against subtle but pervasive age bias on the part
of prospective employers.

Kansas Is Long Ago and Far Away

"Okay," you respond. "Granted that I'm dealing with a difficult situation and that the current business picture looks a little rough. Eventually, however, things have got to get back to normal, right?" Don't
count on it.

One of my favorite movies is *The Wizard of Oz*. I love the part when
Dorothy steps out of her house into the land of Oz and says, "Toto, I
don't think we're in Kansas anymore." It's time for us to realize that
as managers, we too left Kansas a long time ago. When the dust finally
settles and our little house stops spinning, we are going to look around
and realize that things will never be the same again.

Several key business factors suggest that the future is likely to be
fraught with job insecurity, high work stress, and excessive demands.
To begin with, as long as medical benefits and pension plans continue
to consume a disproportionate amount of corporate profits, every organization is going to find itself under continuing pressure to look for
creative ways to increase its productivity while reducing employee
costs. Companies will do this by continuing to off-shore jobs to other
countries, expanding their use of contract workers and part-time employees, and raising the efficiency of their core processes. For example,
more than 90 percent of the 365,000 jobs that were created during the
month of February 1993 were part-time positions.[3] As companies attempt "re-engineering" efforts aimed at the wholesale elimination of
nonproductive functions and processes, the economy is likely to lose
an additional 1.5 to 2 million jobs each year for a period of several
years.[4]

These factors suggest that even if U.S. productivity rises and
profits increase, there is likely to be little rebound on jobs. The job
growth that does occur will be quickly absorbed by the millions of
underemployed workers who have been forced to accept jobs outside
their professional fields. Another factor will be the ongoing large-scale
displacement of workers in the military and in defense industries. According to the Bureau of Labor Statistics, military contractors will eliminate an estimated three hundred thousand jobs by 1997, and additional reductions by their suppliers may generate the loss of another
million jobs.[5]

As companies strive to remain lean, those who remain employed will find themselves under unrelenting pressure to show that they provide substantial "value-added" to their organizations. Managers in particular will find that their organizations are scrutinizing them carefully to see if they are able to adapt quickly and successfully to the new business challenges confronting them.

Enter the New Job Survivalist

Faced with these challenges, some professionals choose to take a relatively passive stance to their jobs. Confused about how to respond to the stresses of job insecurity and excessive work demands, they tend to withdraw or give up. Others become embittered and angry, assuming that there is little they can do to safeguard their jobs. Still others, however, are discovering that they are not helpless and that they can take innovative steps to secure their jobs and advance their careers. For want of a better term, I refer to such individuals as the new job survivalists. What sets these job survivalists apart from other professionals? In what ways are they different? Before I answer these questions, take a few minutes to take the Job Survival Quiz (see below). The quiz consists of six situations. For each situation, you will be asked to do two things:

- First, use a 1-to-10 rating scale to indicate the degree of difficulty that you would have in managing each situation. A score of 1 means no problem; a score of 10 means extremely problematic.
- Second, show how you would respond to each situation by selecting one of four available responses. Be honest with yourself, and select responses that are most typical of your management style.

Later in this chapter, you will be provided with a scoring key for interpreting your results.

The Job Survival Quiz

1. You begin to hear rumors that your organization will soon be expanding into a new market area. If this rumor is true, it would greatly expand your team's range of responsibilities and also require the introduction of new technical skills.
   - How would you rate this situation? _____

- How would you respond to this situation?
  a. Systematically scan reliable sources in your organization for information that can help you confirm these rumors.
  b. Wait to see what happens. This sort of rumor has occurred before and is often without basis.
  c. Take the initiative by confronting your manager and explaining that your team is now dealing with as much work as it can handle and can't afford to branch out into a new area.
  d. Put together a list of questions about the rumor and pose them at your next quarterly department meeting, which will be held two months from now.

2. As a result of a new organizational productivity improvement effort your team has been pushed to the limits, and its members appear stressed out and fatigued.
   - How would you rate this situation?   _____
   - How would you respond to this situation?
     a. Tell the team members that although you share their resentment over the new productivity effort, there is nothing that you or they can do about it.
     b. Act as if nothing is wrong, under the assumption that if you don't feed the stress problem a lot of attention, things will quickly revert to normal.
     c. Wait until the team members approach you with their concerns and let you know the type of help they need.
     d. Take steps to coach them in how to manage high-stress situations and reduce any needless stress that you may be creating through your management style.

3. Your team is being swamped by work overload and is having difficulty determining where to focus its efforts.
   - How would you rate this situation?   _____
   - How would you respond to this situation?
     a. Explain to your manager that you are overwhelmed and can't move forward until your manager establishes clear priorities on your projects.
     b. From all of your activities and outputs, take steps to isolate those projects with the greatest value to your internal customers and your manager.
     c. Tell your team members to do what they can and not to worry about those responsibilities that fall behind.
     d. Continue working the way that you have been in the past,

and explain to your internal customers that any delays or problems are caused by your managers' inability to sort out their priorities.

4. During the last two years far fewer merit increases and promotional opportunities have been available for your staff. These factors, along with the grueling hours your team is putting in, have left members somewhat demoralized.

   - How would you rate this situation? _____
   - How would you respond to this situation?
     a. Call your team members together and explain that although you know their motivation is low, your past experience with your company suggests that if they can just wait things out for a year or so, the situation will get back to normal and they will have the rewards they are looking for.
     b. Search for creative methods for making their jobs more challenging, interesting, and enjoyable.
     c. Remind members that you are willing to talk with them if they have any job or career concerns, and then wait for them to take the lead.
     d. Tell members to stop bellyaching and to appreciate the fact that in the current work environment, they are lucky to have a job.

5. As part of your company's cost-cutting and downsizing program, it looks as if you are likely to lose some critical staff members.

   - How would you rate this situation? _____
   - How would you respond to this situation?
     a. Complain loudly to your management that if you don't have sufficient staff to meet your goals, you won't be able to meet your performance objectives.
     b. Get on with your work, with the idea that you will probably have to eventually make some workload adjustments if the downsizing occurs.
     c. Begin to develop a contingency plan that would enable you to make the best use of available staff and capture additional sources of help should the downsizing go into effect.
     d. Hope that your management comes to its senses and realizes that you can't perform without additional staff.

6. As pressures continue to mount in your organization, relationships are beginning to deteriorate between your team and other departments. Specifically, your company's marketing manager

has been reluctant to release to your team certain information and documentation that you need to carry out your function.

- How would you rate this situation?   _____
- How would you respond to this situation?
  a. Casually drop a hint to the marketing manager that you would be willing to sit down and talk.
  b. Make sure your back is covered by going to your own manager, explaining the situation from your point of view and providing detailed documentation on the problems the marketing manager has been creating for your group.
  c. Do nothing. The marketing manager probably knows the political realities of the situation as well as you do and will eventually realize that in-fighting between the two of you can only hurt both your teams.
  d. Outline the situation as you see it to the other manager and ask this individual to help you better understand how he or she views the problem.

The Change Management Model

Before I show you how to score and interpret your responses to the Job Survival Quiz, I need to introduce the Change Management Model, shown in the accompanying figure. This model provides a simple way of looking at four different behavioral approaches to change.

The model comprises two dimensions. The vertical dimension refers to an individual's focus of control. People who adopt a *passive* approach to change tend to react and respond to situations, rather than take the initiative. These are people who sit in the passenger seat of life's car, waiting to be driven to their destination. Because much of their attention centers on causal factors that are directly outside their control and understanding, they see themselves as passively driven by the larger forces surrounding them and as being able to exert only limited control over their lives. By contrast, people who are *active* tend to focus on those aspects of their work environments and personal lives that are within their direct control and strive to take charge of their lives. These are people who see themselves as causal agents in their own lives. They place themselves firmly in the driver's seat and actively chart their own destination and path.

The horizontal dimension of the model refers to an individual's focus in time. *Past-focused* people are stuck in time. They tend to ignore

The Change Management Model

	Focus of Time	
	Past	**Future**
Active	**Resistive** • Opposes change. • Complains. • Poisons the well. • Casts blame, seeks a prosecutor.	**Preemptive** • Anticipates change. • Tests the limits. • Aggressively seeks information. • Focuses on the doables.
Passive	**Retrospective** • Denies change. • Responds from habit. • Withdraws and retreats. • Ignores new information, minimizes problems.	**Reactive** • Responds late in the change process. • Waits for direction. • Seeks a rescuer. • Accommodates rather than adapts to change.

Focus of Control

or resist change and attempt to navigate by looking in the rearview mirror. They cling with anger or remorse to the past, continually missing important warning signs or opportunity markers that lie in front of them. In contrast, people who are *future-focused* are able to separate events that are fixed and unchangeable from those that are open to review. As a result, they are able to let go of the past and focus on the future. Although they may occasionally glance in the rearview mirror to gain perspective, the bulk of their attention is focused on their destination.

Together, these two dimensions—focus of control and focus of time—form four different approaches to change, which I call *resistive, retrospective, reactive,* and *preemptive.*

1. *Resistive* people actively oppose change and have to be dragged, kicking and screaming, into the future. When faced with a new challenge, they may respond by complaining about their problems or by casting blame on others: "If it weren't for him, we never would have been in this mess!" Still another response is to "poison the well"—to sabotage change efforts intentionally in order to keep others from benefiting from these changes or to reverse or delay the change process.

2. *Retrospective* people also have difficulty dealing with the future. Unlike resistive people, however, they handle their anxiety by denying change ("The reorganization probably won't go through") or by minimizing the likely impact of change ("Things won't be as bad as you think"). People who use this change management approach sometimes fail to adapt successfully to new work situations because they insist on applying tried-and-true approaches to new demands. In doing so, they often ignore information that could help them master these new challenges.

3. *Reactive* people are focused on the future but take a passive position with regard to change. They often fail to react to new events until they are deeply immersed in the change. A key part of their response to change involves looking for someone—their manager, a friend, or an associate—who can serve as a rescuer and who can provide needed guidance and support. They interpret taking the initiative as "going to my manager to ask for assistance or direction." They tend to respond to change by acclimating themselves to change rather than by using adaptive behavior to manage the speed and direction of change.

4. *Preemptive* people are true job survivors; they don't waste time complaining about events that are already history or reminiscing about

"the good old days." These individuals are able to deal with the present on its own terms. They know that work success depends on being able to remain flexible and to readily adapt to ever-changing and unpredictable work conditions. As a result, they aggressively seek out information that can help them anticipate large-scale organizational and business changes even though these changes are still in their formative stages. In addition, they focus their attention on the "doable," those aspects of their environment that are directly within their range of their control.

Interpreting Your Response Scores

You can use the scoring key shown in the accompanying figure to interpret your scores on the Job Survival Quiz and to determine which of the four management change approaches most closely characterizes your personal management style. To interpret your scores, simply circle the letters on the scoring key that correspond to your answers, and then total your score for each column. Your scores will probably include some responses from each of the four change management approaches, but most of your responses are likely to cluster within one category. This is the approach that you rely on when you find yourself faced with difficult work challenges.

The Quiz Scoring Key				
Situation	Resistive	Retrospective	Reactive	Pre-emptive
1.	c	b	d	a
2.	a	b	c	d
3.	d	c	a	b
4.	d	a	c	b
5.	a	d	b	c
6.	b	c	a	d

1. *For the resistive person:* In attempting to apply the job survival strategies outlined in this book, your personal challenge will be to see if you can adapt a different mind-set and free yourself up from angrily holding on to the past. As you read the chapters, ask yourself, "Will this action help me take care of myself in the future? How will focusing my attention on this help me a year from now?"

2. *For the retrospective person:* As a potential job survivalist, your greatest personal challenge will be to acknowledge the impact of change. This means recognizing that the many disruptive organizational changes you are encountering are not just temporary aberrations but reflect permanent and substantial changes in your workplace. As you progress through this book, consider using a trusted associate—one who can remain somewhat detached—as a reality check to provide you with an objective view of your work situation and to offer new and innovative approaches to problems.

3. *For the reactive person:* Your greatest personal challenge involves learning how to leap ahead of change and tackle it before it overwhelms you. In addition, you will need to rely more on your own initiative and less on the direction and advice of others. As you read this book, try to keep in mind that many of the challenges now facing your organization represent unprecedented problems for your managers and associates. As a result, they may not be able to provide you with quick and easy cookie-cutter solutions to your problems. Ask yourself, "To what degree am I willing to take the initiative on resolving emerging work problems? To what extent am I willing to rely on my own personal resources and judgment in effecting change in my organization?"

4. *For the preemptive person:* If you are preemptive, you should find it easier to apply the managerial survival strategies outlined in this book. Before you rush off to celebrate, however, perform a quick reality check on your answers. Give the Job Survival Quiz to someone who is well acquainted with your performance and ask him to indicate the responses he feels are typical of your change management style. Don't be surprised if his answers are somewhat different from your own.

As a preemptive person, the greatest personal challenge you face is maintaining your adaptive approach to change, despite occasionally being beaten back by difficult work situations or surrounded by others who believe that there is little you (or they) can do to manage change successfully. Don't believe them. Keep your attention firmly focused on the path in front of you, on those elements of change that are firmly within your control.

Six Managerial Challenges

The six situations presented in the Job Survival Quiz correspond to today's six greatest management challenges, which are summarized in the figure on page 16. In the Your Rating column, record the importance score you gave each situation in the quiz, and then review the following chapter summaries to determine how you would like to proceed through this book.

Challenge 1. Develop a Fast Draw. Cycle time and fast response are quickly closing in on quality improvement as today's most important performance standards. Many managers are being challenged to improve their response time within work settings that are increasingly confusing, disconnected, and chaotic. The skill of "developing a fast draw" means learning how to deliver the fastest possible response to your manager and to your internal and external customers by scanning your organization for changes that could affect your team, establishing early-warning systems to alert you to potential problem areas, and strengthening communication links between members.

Challenge 2. Banish Bedlam and Burnout. Excessive work stress can seriously limit your team's performance. In this chapter we present ways to help your team "banish bedlam and burnout" by identifying the symptoms of stress overload and by taking steps to help your staff manage high-stress situations. In addition, we explain how your management style may be creating needless stress and anxiety in your team and steps you can take to modify stress-generating behavior.

Challenge 3. Focus Efforts. During periods of rapid organizational change, it's often difficult to sort out priorities and target key work issues. Most of us tend to solve these problems by looking inward and by taking our clues from those people who work closely with us on a day-to-day basis. The strategy of "focusing efforts" shows you how to step outside this limited field of view by using customer feedback to map your team's performance. In this chapter we also describe how to select those work improvements options that have the greatest chance of success.

Challenge 4. Inspire the Troops. It's easy to motivate others if your business is growing by leaps and bounds, promotional opportunities are unlimited, and financial incentives are easily available. The real challenge comes when employees are expected to improve their performance dramatically at the same time that these traditional carrot-and-stick incentives are suddenly taken away. The skill of "inspiring

The Chapters and the Challenges

Situation	Your Rating	Challenge	Chapter
1.	—	• Developing the skill of rapid deployment	1. *Develop a Fast Draw*
2.	—	• Helping your team manage stress overload	2. *Banish Bedlam and Burnout*
3.	—	• Determining priorities and direction for your team	3. *Focus Efforts*
4.	—	• Motivating in the new work environment	4. *Inspire the Troops*
5.	—	• Matching your human resources to your requirements	5. *Close Ranks and Reform*
6.	—	• Developing an internal support network and minimizing conflicts with other groups	6. *Forge Alliances*

the troops" will help you overcome team inertia by providing members with support and encouragement during tough times, making members fully accountable for performance, and recharging the batteries of teams that are beaten down and demoralized. Another section of this chapter deals with how to motivate and challenge yourself to greater work efforts.

Challenge 5. Close Ranks and Reform. A common problem confronting many managers these days is how to get their objectives accomplished when they find themselves faced with staff reductions. In this chapter we discuss how to obtain the best efforts from available staff and how to obtain surrogate help for your team. You will be introduced to tools that can help you obtain better work coverage through the reassignment of staff. We also help you deal with the opposite challenge—having excess staff. We describe how to find alternative uses for excess staff, how to build a strong case to your management regarding your need for staff, and how to take steps to minimize the impact of staff reductions.

Challenge 6. Forge Alliances. One of the first things that usually happens when organizations begin to encounter tough times is that interdepartmental teamwork begins to break down as groups scramble for limited resources and staff and seek to redirect performance pressure away from themselves and toward other groups. Without strong alliances you are more vulnerable to disruptive changes and cut yourself off from important networks of influence and information. In this chapter we present the principles of positive politics, show you how to determine where your team lies in your organization's political network, and introduce several tools you can use for building interteam relationships and for resolving conflicts with other groups. This information will help you develop the allies you need to accomplish your objectives.

The six management skills we've just described can provide you with the strategies, tactics, and tools you need to master the difficult management challenges that lie ahead. Use your rating scores to determine the sequence in which you approach the remaining chapters (you can tackle them in any order) and the relative degree of emphasis you should place on each chapter.

As you read through this book, keep in mind that perhaps the most important characteristic in determining which managers will survive and thrive in the next few years and which will fall by the wayside is tenacity. Take the time to carefully read the chapters, work through the Took Kit in each chapter, and you will find that your investment of time and effort will be amply repaid in the future.

Notes

1. Al Ehrbar, " 'Re-Engineering' Gives Firms New Efficiency, Workers the Pink Slip," *The Wall Street Journal* (March 16, 1993), p. 1.
2. Ceel Pasternak, "Update: Getting Older," *HRMagazine* (May 1990), p. 27.
3. Jack Gordon, "Into the Dark: Rough Ride Ahead for American Workers," *Training Magazine* (July 1993), pp. 21–29.
4. Ehrbar, " 'Re-Engineering,' " p. 1.
5. Louis S. Richman, "When Will the Layoffs End?" *Fortune* (September 20, 1993), pp. 54–56. © 1993, Time, Inc. All rights reserved.

The Challenges

Challenge 1
Develop a Fast Draw

Rapidly Responding to Change

If one thing is clear, it's that rapid, disruptive change has become a fact of life. Every organization, whether it is in the field of medical care, hospitality management, or computer manufacturing, is beginning to realize that a key to survival will be the ability to rapidly respond to large-scale changes. At the organization level, this need translates into the concept of time-based competition and is achieved by finding ways to streamline key work processes. At the team level, quick response means being able to mobilize your team efficiently to respond to sudden changes in your workplace. Like a gunslinger from the Wild West, you need to develop a fast draw to stay one jump ahead of the competition. In today's unpredictable work environment, your survival and success depends upon it. To achieve a rapid response, you must be able to overcome three interrelated problems.

Poor Long-Range Vision

Within fast-paced organizations, it is essential to anticipate any large-scale changes that could severely affect your team's performance. When teams can't tell where their organizations are headed, the result is often a high level of fear and anxiety. Patrick Miller, director of human resources for TECO Transport and Trade, provides this explanation: "A major cause of stress is team members' feeling that the organization is evolving in ways which are mysterious and that they don't understand the forces behind the scene that are driving organizational change. They feel that they are being taken to an unknown destination and don't know if they will like that destination."[1]

Several factors drive the problem of poor long-range vision. First, organizations sometimes fail to carefully integrate organizational changes, such as new product entries or total quality programs, into their overall business strategies. If this is occurring in your company, senior managers may be hard pressed to explain how those changes relate to the organization's vision statement so proudly displayed in the corporate lobby. Second, senior managers may not even be aware of some of the important changes now under way. Finally, managers are often reluctant to disclose information on traumatic changes such as major reorganizations or downsizings on the grounds that such information could adversely affect performance.

For these reasons, in many cases you may have only limited access to information on important organizational changes and will need to rely on your own devices to keep abreast of changes that could affect your team's performance. In this chapter you will learn how to "sniff the wind" to obtain information on large-scale organizational changes.

Sporadic Brushfires

The second problem you face in attempting to mobilize your team for quick response is being able to anticipate and efficiently resolve recurring performance problems. This can be particularly taxing if your resources are currently stretched to the limit or if your group has been forced to assume a much broader range of responsibilities. Like a fire-fighting team faced with an outbreak of brushfires, your team members will need to be able to mobilize quickly for action and to deploy themselves in the most effective manner.

To deal with this problem, your team members must feel safe enough to expose problems whenever they encounter them, without fear of criticism or reprisal. They must also develop ways to keep one another alerted to the onset of problems. The strategy of creating early-warning systems offers a tactic for meeting this problem.

Communication Breakdowns

The third problem you may face is maintaining effective day-to-day communication with your team members. Communication breakdowns have a tendency to increase as teams tackle tougher workloads and members become scattered among different projects or are spread across different sites.

If your organization is experiencing tough times, other communication problems come into play. Some members may pull back into their protective shells in the belief that if they isolate themselves they will be less exposed to risk and criticism. When professionals are exposed to high-risk changes such as downsizings or reorganizations, they often shift much of their energy from productive work to searching for information that can help them recalibrate their safety level within the new organizational structure.

The flip side of this problem is that during times of turbulent change you need to audit your own communication style, as there is a natural tendency for everyone, managers and team members alike, to become more withdrawn and isolated when exposed to work stress. You will be introduced to tactics for addressing this problem when we discuss the strategy of tightening communication links.

The Challenges in Perspective

These three interrelated problems—poor long-range vision, sporadic brushfires, and communication breakdowns—affect the company at different levels, from organizationwide communications to day-to-day team interactions. By discovering ways to address all three problems successfully, you can make certain that your team is able to address external problems and challenges quickly and effectively.

Warning Symptoms

The following warning symptoms can help you determine whether the need for rapid response is a significant performance challenge for your team. Check off those symptoms you've observed in your own team.

- ❑ Information about serious company problems is difficult to obtain, is unreliable, or is available only through the rumor mill.
- ❑ Your team appears to be "slow on the draw" and frequently encounters costly time delays when attempting to respond to problems.
- ❑ On several occasions your team has been caught off guard by changes or problems that you should have seen coming.
- ❑ The members of your team appear closed off and uncommunicative. You feel that you have to pry information out of them.
- ❑ Team members seem to have difficulty responding to problems unless they are provided with close direction and guidance.

Strategies

The starting point for setting direction and focusing team efforts is to "sniff the wind" for clues that can alert you to large-scale organizational changes. This strategy also involves determining how these changes are likely to affect your team and helping team members align their efforts with your organization's overall direction.

The second strategy involves identifying performance areas in which your team has encountered recurring problems and developing methods by which team members can warn one another of the onset of these problems. This, in turn, means that you have to create an environment in which members aren't afraid to disclose performance problems and are able to respond quickly and decisively to the outbreak of problems without depending on you.

The final strategy is based on enhancing day-to-day communication within your team. A useful tactic here is to use communication technology to help members keep one another better informed. Another tactic involves clearing a path up the line to keep the attention of your senior managers focused on emerging problems and work issues. Finally, realizing that time pressure is often a limiting factor in establishing good team communications, we suggest a third tactic that involves exploring time-limited communication methods, such as the use of stand-up meetings and brown-bag lunches.

Strategy 1: Sniff the Wind

• **Track what gets attended to.** The easiest way to track your organization's direction is to look at what gets attended to and rewarded in your organization. This tactic follows the old adage that actions speak louder than words, or, as one of our client's employees aptly put it, "When we want to find out which way our company is headed, we watch our managers' feet, not their lips."

If you want to watch your managers' feet, start with the area of agenda visibility. Executives, like most people, tend to put their time where their hearts are. Having trouble getting in to see your manager? Look over his secretary's shoulder the next time she scans through his appointment book, and sneak a quick peek at where your manager is spending his time. This provides a strong clue as to his priorities.

Ask your manager for a copy of the summary or minutes of the last few executive staff meetings, and note the percentage of time that was allocated to different issues. How many meetings were devoted to discussions of problems with customers? How many focused on new programs with suppliers? What about new human resources initiatives or changes in corporate policy? The flip side of this strategy is to pay attention to those issues that are repeatedly bumped from the agenda.

• **Track paths of influence.** Still another technique for spotting emerging organizational changes involves tracking shifting players and responsibilities. Make a list of ten senior-level managers who are considered to be strongly influential in your organization. Have these individuals been recently reassigned? Where to? These are the areas you need to track. On the other hand, by repositioning functions under mediocre performers, management sends a strong signal that these functions are perceived to be noncritical.

• **Identify your organization's "Sunday best."** When I was a child, it was a common practice to set aside your best pair of shoes and suit of clothes—your "Sunday best"—from the rest of your wardrobe and save them for the most important occasions. Every organization has its Sunday best—those functions and programs that are paraded out to impress customers and the top corporate officers. These areas change on a regular basis. Yesterday's showpiece becomes today's mediocre function.

Now think about your own organization for a minute. What functions and programs have recently been:

• Highlighted in your division's annual status report to your corporate office?
• Shown off at your last interdivisional conference?
• Given favorable press by the media (and included in your company's standard press kit)?
• Included in your company's "brag sheets" for its customers?
• Periodically written up in your company's newsletter or video report?
• Considered a mandatory part of any facility tour conducted for visiting VIPs?

These are the change areas that need to be carefully tracked in your company.

• **Determine what gets rewarded.** Ask to see your manager's yearly objectives for the past three years (I'm sure she has them filed away somewhere). As yearly objectives at the department and division level are weighed according to priority, with some objectives given as little as 5 percent weight and others as much as 50 percent, a useful tracking mechanism is to look for shifts in the relative weights that have been assigned to different objectives.

In addition, people focus their efforts on what they get paid for. Which of your manager's objectives or projects are tied to the largest share of her incentive compensation bonus? Once again, more than likely a few key work areas make up the lion's share of this package.

Finally, take a close look at where budgets are growing and shrinking in your organization. If the budget of one function continues to grow despite an official organizationwide budget freeze, that should alert you to the fact that management considers that function critical to its survival.

• **Track shifts in skill emphasis.** Another way of identifying emerging changes in your organization is to look for shifts in skill emphasis.

Which skills are increasingly rewarded in your company? Which are becoming less important? The human resources managers of one company consistently informed their engineering employees that they considered a master's degree in engineering to be more valuable than an M.B.A. Despite this official position, a review of the company's blue sheets listing the bios of recently promoted managers showed that there was a strong tendency to promote M.B.A. graduates over individuals who had received master's degrees in engineering.

In what areas is your company beginning to spend big bucks on training? Ask your human resources manager for a list of training courses and off-site seminars, and observe where the money goes.

What new technologies or product areas are being carefully monitored by your organization? Are individuals who have unique technical skills being aggressively recruited by your company? Changes in your company's technical skill mix may signal your organization's initial involvement in emerging markets or different technologies. When you have an opportunity, make a list of those technical skills that you feel are becoming more important in your organization, and compare this list with similar lists developed by your associates. You may be surprised at what you find.

• **Track your organizational pioneers.** Some managers and groups respond faster than others to change. These individuals pride themselves on being able to anticipate accurately emerging trends and strive to be at the leading edge of organizational change. Who are your organizational pioneers? Take the time to invite one of them, or a member of their staff, out to lunch, and find out where these pioneers are now focusing their attention.

• **Peer through the looking glass.** Another way to gauge large-scale changes is to find out how your organization is viewed from the outside. For example, pay close attention to the consultants being brought in by your organization. Some consulting companies perform 90 percent of their work in the areas of downsizing operations and cost reduction projects, while others work almost exclusively on total quality management or team building. Discovering the types of consulting companies that are being courted by your senior management can give you strong clues as to the performance issues that are being carefully monitored in the executive suite.

In addition, suppliers and customers often know about key organizational changes before this information is released to employees. Make it a point to have personal contact with some of your most important external suppliers and customers, and invite their feedback regarding recent changes that they've noted in your organization.

Finally, keep abreast of information on your company's performance as featured in leading business and technical journals. Pay particular attention to those performance areas (quality products, customer satisfaction, community responsiveness) about which your organization is especially sensitive as it protects its corporate image. If you don't have time to read several journals or periodicals, at least scan your local library's *Guide to Business Periodicals* or electronic data base periodically to locate, by subject area, recent articles on your company's business performance.

- **Identify what's sensitive to the touch.** Performance areas that are extremely sensitive to the touch are closely tracked by senior management and receive the lion's share of attention from your company. To find out what's sensitive, ask yourself:

  - In what performance areas does failure carry the greatest risk?
  - In what performance areas are senior managers beginning to micromanage functions and tighten controls or exercise extreme caution before signing off on decisions?
  - What information is tightly controlled and released on a need-to-know basis?
  - In what areas do people immediately jump on problems and take decisive action? In what areas do people routinely ignore performance problems or fail to live up to performance commitments?

- **Observe your organizational mirrors.** Every organization measures its progress against that of certain other companies. This assessment may take the form of:

  - Performing formal benchmarking studies involving world-class achievers in your field
  - Attempting to duplicate change initiatives that have been successfully undertaken by companies that are admired by your organization
  - Following in the footsteps of a group at another company that

has achieved a solid reputation for taking the lead on innovative change

- Moving toward change as the result of tracking your competitors' moves

I know of one defense contractor that, despite strong signs of a rapidly shrinking military market, steadfastly refused to explore entering the commercial market until it saw its primary competitor move in this direction. Which organizations does your company track? What moves are these organizations making that your company may soon replicate? How can you track these moves? If, for example, your organizational mirror is another company division, you might attempt to locate someone within that division who could serve as a reliable source of information on important changes. In the same way, you could take steps to track your competitors' moves by:

- Buying your competitors' products, breaking them down, and analyzing the cost of production or advanced design features in these products.
- Stalking your competitor's territory by establishing inroads into your competitors' social, professional, and business networks.
- Employing a clipping service to search for articles pertaining to your competitors.
- Obtaining information on your competitor through one of the available computerized information services, such as the *Dow Jones News Retrieval Service* or the *New York Times Information Bank*. In addition, you can obtain copies of speeches by corporate executives to financial analysts and of assessments of corporations by brokerage firms through the *Wall Street Transcript*. If you want to keep abreast of information on newly patented material, *The Official Gazette* might prove helpful.[2]

You've now been introduced to nine methods for tracking important trends, both within and without your organization, that could significantly affect your work team. The Change Analysis Chart in the Tool Kit is useful for consolidating information on major changes.

Strategy 2: Create Early-Warning Systems

- **Target a few key performance areas for tracking.** A mistake frequently made by managers is to attempt to track everything, regardless of its importance. As an alternative approach, I suggest that you are better off developing a very thorough performance tracking system that focuses on no more than three performance areas. These areas should be:

- *Critical*—Important to both your department and function and your external or internal customers. The Performance Map in Challenge 3 may be helpful in identifying key performance areas.
- *Volatile*—Likely to cycle out of control and be subject to wide variations in performance.
- *High risk*—Strongly associated with team success and carrying with them high risks for failure.
- *Urgent*—Frequently requiring a rapid response from your team.
- *Invisible*—Often hidden from view, either because they are created upstream of your team or because they are outside of your team's direct field of observation.
- *Problematic*—Often taking your team by surprise.

- **Use visual control systems to track performance trends.** If they are carefully designed, visual control systems can provide clear, easily interpretable feedback on your team's current performance. These systems should:

- Include a clearly marked target level for performance, based on data from either historical performance or benchmarked companies
- Be based on data that are accurate and timely
- Be fairly simple to generate and update
- Be located in areas that are easily accessible by members

Two ways in which visual control systems can be used as early-warning systems are illustrated by the Project Milestone Chart (Figure 1-1) and the Team Transition Chart discussed in Challenge 5.

- **Establish results and process performance measures.** When we think of tracking performance, we usually think of ways to track end results. For a sales manager a key results measure might be total dollar sales volume; for a purchasing manager it might be cycle time and error rates for purchase orders. Although results measures do provide us with a quantifiable bottom line assessment of performance, they have several drawbacks:

- They place you in a reactive position. Do you really want to wait until you encounter customer complaints (or, worse yet, lose sales) to learn about problems you are having with your internal and external customers?
- They create delays in performance improvement. Extended

Figure 1-1. The Project Milestone Chart.

Potential Roadblocks	Degree of Problem	PHASE I	WEEK 1	WEEK 2	WEEK 3	WEEK 4	WEEK 5	WEEK 6
		Stage 1						
Step 1 Smith is critical of project. Could derail exec. review. Ask director to meet w/him to gain commitment.	● (Critical)	Step 1	Process Analysis Training; Executive Review; Team Review & Kick-off					
Step 2 Respondents may be fearful of giving honest feedback. Suggest taking interviews offsite.	◗ (Moderate)	Step 2	Employee Involvement Survey Distributed & Analyzed (Optional)		Performance Assessment Questionnaires Designed, Distributed & Analyzed; Performance Assessment Interviews	Performance Assessment Report		
Step 3 Will other division release benchmarking data? Ask Bill to contact them and get info.	◔ (Minor)	Step 3			Review of Benchmarking Data	Benchmarking Site Visits; Prepare Comparative Benchmarking Report		
Step 4 Need directors' upfront agreement on cost-benefit analysis criteria.	◕ (Significant)	Step 4					Cost/Benefit Analysis Review; Prepare Cost/Benefit Analysis Report	
Step 5 None.		Step 5						Recommendations Rpt.; Exec. Review

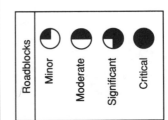

Roadblocks

◔	Minor
◗	Moderate
◕	Significant
●	Critical

lapses between the time of the team's actual performance and time you receive feedback from your customers means that it takes you longer to put corrective actions into place.

- They encourage the problem to grow out of control. The longer the time lag between the occurrence of a performance problem and the receipt of feedback on that problem, the more the problem has a chance to spread.
- They may tell you *how well* you are doing, but they don't provide a lot of detailed information about *why* you are encountering performance problems.

For all these reasons, the most effective early-warning systems supplement results measures with the use of process measures—measures of performance on key activities that are directly related to end results. For example, a sales manager discovered that her team's sales volume had steadily declined over the last six months, despite the recent addition of several new products by her company. To pinpoint the cause of this problem and to develop a tracking system for spotting its occurrence in the future, she should collect data on several key process measures that have been shown to correspond to sales volume.

You are probably saying to yourself, "But I don't have time to review a lot of numbers each week!" The answer to this problem is to use certain (primary) process indicators as triggers for determining whether you need to probe further into selected performance areas. If you do, you can then move on to a review of additional (secondary) indicators. This may sound confusing, but you probably perform this type of two-stage analysis every day of your life. For example, if your car refuses to start, you could immediately perform a diagnosis of your entire electrical system. As a practical matter, however, you would probably first try to take some simple, exploratory steps such as checking to see if your horn and headlights work in order to determine whether your battery is dead. Similarly, your annual physical exam contains a few standard primary indicators—blood pressure and heart readings, for example—that can alert your doctor to the possibility of problems requiring more detailed examination.

You can see from these simple examples that primary indicators serve as "advance scouts"; they nudge you and invite you to look further. Some of the primary and secondary process indicators that could be used by our hypothetical sales manager are shown in the Performance Analysis Chart in Figure 1-2.

Figure 1-2. Example of a Performance Analysis Chart.

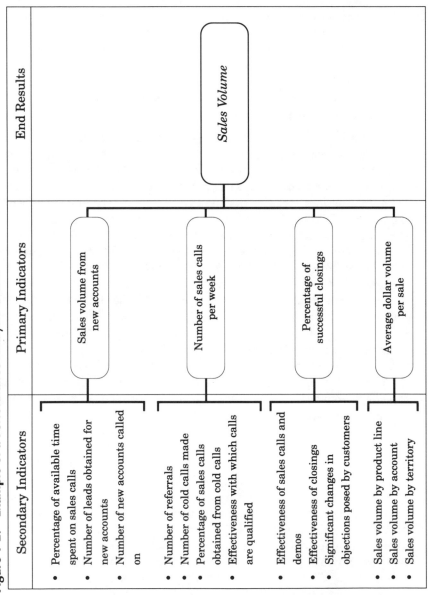

• **For project plans, pinpoint areas of potential risk.** One useful tactic is to break apart project plans in order to identify those steps that involve excessive risk and that require careful monitoring by your team. Functions such as product development and proposal teams, which may apply the same project planning model to a variety of projects, may find a "lessons learned" file to be another useful tool. This personal notebook on obstacles, shortcuts, and other lessons learned by team members from their experiences with previous projects can be used to identify potential pitfalls on new projects. Challenge 3's Project Planning Worksheet can help you identify potential problems associated with each project step and take preventive and corrective actions for coping with these problems.

• **Red-flag repeated performance problems.** Another tactic is to use a special filing or coding system to track past problem areas that need to be handled carefully. As an example, one major hotel chain maintains a data base on past customers. When a guest calls in for a reservation and the guest's name is entered into the hotel's computer, the computer screen displays any particular complaints or special requests that have been previously noted by the customer. If, for example, a customer is a light sleeper and has previously complained about being placed in a noisy location, the employee making the reservation knows not to give the customer a room next to the ice machine or the hotel lounge.

Although many managers claim to have established red-flag systems, these systems are often ineffective. You can use this list to help you evaluate the effectiveness of your own early-warning systems:

• What percentage of performance areas have you included in your early warning system? Managers sometimes make the mistake of red-flagging everything, which defeats the purpose. If you've flagged more than 10 percent of your activities for monitoring, this indicates that you are having trouble distinguishing between critical and noncritical activities.

• How far in advance does your system alert you to problems? After all, a smoke alarm isn't very effective if it comes on only after a fire is blazing out of control. In the same way, it doesn't help you to know that certain customers are easily irritated by a certain performance issue thirty minutes into a phone call with them.

• Is your system updated on a routine basis?

• Are your red flags easy to distinguish and unambiguous? Although my fuel gauge shows how low the gas in my car is getting, the use of a separate "empty" light placed close to eye level helps to ensure that I don't ignore the warning. That's the beauty of color-coded file systems—they help to redirect your attention to the problem at hand.

• **Empower team members to make timely midcourse corrections.** It doesn't do any good to develop an early warning system if team members are forced to sit on their hands while they wait for you to take care of problems. Not long ago, my company received a form letter from the contract manager in one of our customer organizations claiming that our company had failed to provide adequate evidence of insurance coverage. The letter said that our contract was in jeopardy unless we provided this information within ten working days. Our records, however, indicated that this information had already been submitted several months earlier. What followed was a frustrating period of several days in which we attempted to contact the contract manager and were unable to do so. What was most frustrating, however, was that no one else in the contract office was authorized to take action or even had access to the manager's files.

When managers limit their team members' ability to take action on critical problems, they not only hamstring their own effectiveness but severely damage the morale and enthusiasm of their teams.

Use the Empowerment Questionnaire in the Tool Kit to look for ways to improve your team's performance through empowerment.

• **Keep your bow cocked.** A crossbow has two advantages over a longbow. The first is that, being precocked, it can be more quickly released when needed. The second advantage is that the cocking mechanism (a hand-turned crank) relieves part of the pressure on the archer, who is therefore able to take aim without maintaining a lot of force on the bow. In a similar manner, one of the most effective tactics you can use for preparing your team to respond quickly to problems is to keep your bow cocked, that is, to preroute decisions and actions well in advance of when they are needed.

While it's impossible to anticipate every conceivable problem that you could face on a given job or project, it is possible to engage your team in decision scenarios that help refine their ability to think through problems and to make decisions. I know of a sales team that meets regularly to conduct trial runs for planned customer sales calls and to try to anticipate the types of questions or concerns customers are likely to raise. Likewise, an engineering team conducts trial runs to anticipate possible "grenades" that could be thrown at them when they review the status of major engineering projects or discuss the rationale for proposed design changes.

These types of learning scenarios help prime teams for the delivery of quick response, in much the same way that conducting frequent fire drills helps people respond quickly and think clearly when suddenly faced with a fire.

One way to conduct this type of scenario building for your team is to complete the Project Planning Worksheet in Challenge 3 as a team exercise. Another approach is to use the Problem Scenario Exercise in the Tool Kit for this challenge. A third possibility is to develop contingency plans that effectively shuffle members and responsibilities around to accommodate the possible onset of big projects. One of the best examples I can think of involves the writing of my first book, *Lifeboat Strategies*. At the time I began submitting proposals to publishers I had completed only three of the book's twelve chapters. I realized, however, that the timeliness of the book's topic (career survival for nonmanagerial professionals) meant that if it was accepted for publication I would be requested to move quickly on the book's completion. I therefore developed two work scenarios, one based on the assumption that I would be able to spread the writing of the book over the next twelve months (requiring 20 percent of my available time) and the second (which turned out to be correct) based on the assumption that I would need to complete the book over the next few months (requiring 80 percent of my available time). Coming up with the alternatives required reaching agreement with my business partner regarding the types of projects that could be safely offloaded to other people and the types of consulting projects on which our company could successfully bid.

This method of "spring-loading" responsibilities to accommodate different scenarios means that when a large project is suddenly dropped in your lap, you can respond faster, having already undertaken the planning and troubleshooting process. It also means that your team is able to respond effectively to crises. Joe Ferrel, senior planning analyst at Florida Power and Light Company, discussed FPL's response to Hurricane Andrew in 1992 as an excellent example of how to mobilize for rapid deployment.

Joe explained that as a result of careful preparation and planning, FPL was able to restore power to all customers within a month and a half. He suggested that there are six lessons to be learned from FPL's Hurricane Andrew experience:

1. *Preplanning is critical.* You must have a good response plan and well-trained and well-qualified people who have had a chance to practice the plan's execution. FPL

chose to allow employees time away from their normal work to study the system and to prepare for a storm.

2. *Be flexible during the deployment.* Our storm organization was somewhat centralized in its design. This was to ensure that limited resources were being used on the highest priority restoration work. . . . Midway through the restoration effort, we shifted to a more decentralized approach, in which we regionalized our restoration areas. . . . This dramatically reduced the time it took to work on priority areas.

3. *People involved in the deployment must be empowered.* Everyone in the restoration effort knew very well what our objectives were. To achieve those objectives people nearest the field had to have the authority to take reasonable action without the constraint of a bureaucracy. As an example, during the storm our corporate helicopters were destroyed. Recognizing this, someone leased one from North Florida. The aircraft showed up just when the need for an aerial survey became obvious.

4. *People need to adapt to extraordinary conditions.* Andrew destroyed so many buildings and uprooted so many trees that no one could even get close enough to some of our lines to assess the damage. In certain areas tree trimming and debris removal needed to be done before utility personnel were allowed access. We adapted our plans to account for this.

5. *Priorities must be clear and well communicated.* Everyone knew [FPL's] priorities. . . . These priorities drove every decision made by everyone involved in the restoration effort.

6. *Have a clear, unambiguous trigger that mobilizes the response*—a clear red flag that announces the start of the mobilization effort.[3]

For those of you who frequently find yourself in the frustrating situation of hurry-up-and-wait, this tactic can prove quite helpful. If your challenge is to juggle a number of team members and responsibilities in an uncertain work environment, you may also find it useful to review the Team Transition chart in Challenge 5.

Strategy 3: Tighten Communication Links

• **Determine areas of interdependency.** Within any team, communication is most likely to break down in areas in which team members are highly interdependent and require fast responses. A simple way to identify such areas is to invite members to list their major activities and the steps involved in their projects. Then copy the chart in Figure 1-3 onto a flipchart, and ask team members to help you determine where each activity fits on the graph. For example, activities and project steps that require a fast response from your team and that involve a high level of interdependence among team members fall in the upper right-hand quadrant of the chart. Tighten communication links on these activities.

• **Remove fear from the equation.** One of the greatest barriers to quick response is fear. People naturally tend to hide problems if they feel that their organizations are likely to kill messengers carrying bad news. In addition, team members may well feel that if they call your attention to problems they will end up inheriting the responsibility for solving these problems, increasing their own stress levels. Fear plays an even bigger factor in disrupting communications during periods of organizational instability. When companies downsize or reorganize, people feel vulnerable and take whatever measures they can to protect themselves from criticism and overexposure. Typical actions may in-

Figure 1-3. The Interdependency Communication Linkage Chart.

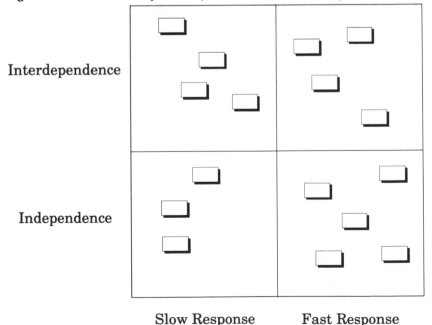

Interdependence

Independence

Slow Response   Fast Response

clude hiding mistakes, waiting to follow your lead rather than taking the initiative on problem solving, delaying action, or taking the safe path and applying makeshift solutions to problems rather than taking the more difficult step of uncovering their root causes.

Any or all of these actions will cause a major slowdown in the reaction time of your team. In extreme cases, they may even cause your team to come to a complete halt. The following are some steps you can take to remove fear from the equation:

• *Set the stage.* Have a brief meeting with team members, and let them know that you truly want their input regarding potential problems. If you can, give a recent example of a situation in which your team was able to respond effectively because a member confronted a problem or pointed out a mistake.

• *Use peer reviews and tag teams.* If you are concerned that team members may be hesitant to confront you directly with problems, require them to conduct informal review and troubleshooting sessions with other members. A similar option is to form tag teams, in which two or more members are jointly assigned to the same project.

• *Provide for individual feedback.* If members are new to the troubleshooting function, recommend that together they complete the Project Planning Worksheet in Challenge 3. If time is at a premium, have the member who has the primary responsibility for the project complete all sections of the worksheet, then forward the chart to the rest of the team for review. Each member can attach notes containing suggestions directly to the chart and then return the chart to the project owner for final review. Many individuals find that one advantage of this approach is that it's less intimidating to members than a team or managerial review.

• *Extend trust to your team.* If you want team members to trust you, show that you trust them. Set aside part of a team meeting to outline a project on which you are working and ask members to function as troubleshooters in helping you spot potential shortfalls in your project. To prime the pump, start off by presenting your own concerns, questions, or areas of uncertainty regarding the project. In addition, be honest and candid about revealing your own mistakes. Let your team know through your actions that you treat problems as learning opportunities.

• *Use reframing.* Sometimes fear becomes a factor in problem identification because of the manner in which managers position problems. To lower the fear level, consider using the following door openers to a team discussion:

"This project looks pretty good. Now, before we move on, can you spot any additional opportunities for improvement?"

"As you know, next week this report will be reviewed by the executive steering committee. I'd like you to help me identify any questions or challenges that we might encounter during this session and some of the steps we could take now to address these questions."

"What's your most optimistic schedule projection for this job? What's your most pessimistic schedule projection? What potential problems could slow down our progress on this job? Can you help me come up with some contingency plans for dealing with these pitfalls?"

• **Audit your communication style.** In my experience as a management consultant and team building facilitator, I have found that the level of fear that members feel about exposing problems or mistakes is closely related to four components of your managerial communication style: trust, openness, responsiveness, and accessibility.

Trust refers to whether members feel that you are honest in your communications and whether your intentions are in the best interest of the team. *Openness* refers to your willingness to consider information that challenges your way of thinking or that contradicts dearly held assumptions. *Responsiveness* involves the degree to which you express an interest in and effectively act on information that is presented to you. *Accessibility* refers not only to your availability on the work site but also to whether members feel that you are approachable at work.

The great irony is that if your communication style is intimidating or disruptive you aren't likely to hear about it directly from your team. Instead, if you want to form a clearer picture of how you interact with your team, try these suggestions:

- Ask one of the stronger members of your team to serve as a troubleshooter and to help you identify specific communication behaviors that work for or against you and the situations in which these behaviors significantly affect your team's performance.
- Ask for feedback from another manager, someone you trust, who has had the opportunity to observe closely your interactions with your team.
- Ask the manager of your company's training department for suggestions on internal courses or outside seminars you could take to learn more about your unique communication style.
- Use the Communications Assessment Survey provided in the Tool Kit to obtain anonymous feedback from team members on your communication style.

• **Develop time-limited communication avenues.** Discuss with your team steps you could take to keep communication lines open without investing a lot of time. My recommendation is to shift from weekly one-hour meetings to more targeted daily meetings of no more than five to ten minutes. Whenever possible, these meetings should occur in the morning, and they should be limited to discussions of significant changes or problems immediately facing the team. A good analogy is the type of quick huddle that football teams engage in before starting each play.

Mark Johnson, quality curriculum manager for AT&T Paradyne, suggests that when conducting such meetings, you should "separate those projects that require a variety of support and assistance from those that can be managed more effectively one-on-one by managers. The same thing goes for determining in advance those people who need to receive copies of information."[4]

As another alternative to traditional meetings, consider starting brown-bag team lunches once a week. Or consider making better use of communication hardware, such as voice mail, electronic mail, and faxes. Joe Dunsmore, senior marketing manager for AT&T Paradyne, offers these guidelines for increasing your effectiveness in these areas:

> [One] thing people can do to make better use of faxes and electronic mail is that most of these systems have the ability to predetermine those groups of people with whom you frequently communicate. If you preset your equipment for these groups, it saves time, and you will be more willing to use electronic communication to spread those small, two-sentence messages that you otherwise wouldn't have bothered with.[5]

At my company, we try to make the most effective use of our pagers. Many pagers display an additional number or two beyond the ten numbers needed for a phone number. We use these extra numbers as a coding system. Through the first number in this sequence, we know the general source of the call (1 = customers; 2 = internal/work; 3 = family/personal; 4 = other). The second number tells us the call's relative degree of urgency (1 = emergency, 2 = call ASAP, 3 = not critical). For anyone who has ever found himself trying to decide whether to run out of a meeting to respond to a pager, this simple system can eliminate a lot of confusion.

Still another option is to use groupware or software packages specifically designed to help teams coordinate project schedules and facilitate team decision making. Brian Chitester, a director of process improvement for Pepsi Cola, uses a combination of well-designed early-warning systems and computer software and hardware to manage a team of six people scattered among six regional offices. Brian tracks his team's performance and programs from the team members' to-do lists on their laptop computers, making real-time changes to their schedules as these changes occur. He also consolidates their work schedules into a single rollout each month, a step that prevents him from overcommitting his team.[6]

• **Clear a path up the line.** So far in this section, I've provided suggestions on how you can establish faster team reponse by enhancing communication links among your team members. Many times, however, the slowdown in response time is created not by the team but by management, which delays responding to requests for action and approval. Getting your manager's attention is even more difficult during times of rapid organizational change, when his or her time is spread among many competing priorities.

To overcome this obstacle, you need to develop a communication approach that makes it easier for your manager to (1) identify emerging work problems and (2) understand the points at which you may need to rely upon him or her for support and assistance. The Project Planning Worksheet in Challenge 3 can provide your manager with a quick overview of how you visualize the estimated time frame, resources, potential problem areas, and problem-solving actions for projects. The Project Milestone Chart mentioned earlier in this challenge provides a different approach to project planning. It includes:

• The use of a milestone chart
• Visual symbols for quickly noting the relative severity of problem areas
• A space for describing the specific types of actions and approval that may be needed by your manager
• An area for estimating the time frame in which these actions and approvals may be required

THE TOOL KIT

Change Analysis Chart

The Change Analysis Chart (Figure 1-4) can be used for tracking large-scale changes in your company or business environment that could directly affect the operation of your team. To apply the chart effectively, you have to be familiar with the two ways to track large-scale changes.

Figure 1-4. The Change Analysis Chart.

Change Event:	
Change Indicators	Your Observation
1. Track what gets attended to. On what topics is attention being focused in executive-led meetings? Where is your manager spending his or her time?	
2. Track paths of influence. To what functions have your most influential managers been reassigned? Which functions have been given to mediocre performers?	

3. Identify your organization's "Sunday Best."
 	
What programs/functions have been:
   Highlighted in your company's newsletter or annual report?
   Paraded in front of customers or the media?	

4. Determine what gets rewarded. What functions receive top priority on your manager's yearly objectives list and are heavily weighted in determining her incentive compensation bonus? In what areas are budgets rapidly growing or shrinking?	
5. Track shifts in skill emphasis. What skill areas are being aggressively sought by your company? What types of technical experts are being recruited? What areas are receiving big bucks for training? What new technologies/products are being monitored?	
6. Track your organizational pioneers. Where are they focusing their attention?	
7. Peer through the looking glass. What consultants are being courted by senior managers? What feedback on changes is coming from suppliers and customers? What is being discussed in business or technical journals?	

8. Identify what's sensitive to the touch.
 	
Which are the areas:
   Of high risk?
   For micro-management/restriction of information?
   Where people quickly jump on problems?	

9. Observe your organizational mirrors.
 	
What does your company track:
   World-class performers?
   Admired companies or competitors?	

Situation 1. Change Event Is Known/Impact Is Unknown

You may know that a change event is going to occur but not know how it will affect your team. To analyze this type of situation, begin by providing in the Change Event space of the chart a brief description of the event based on your preliminary knowledge of it. Your goal is to gather information on how the change event will eventually reveal itself through selected change indicators. For example, if you know that your company will soon be diversifying into a new technology, you may be interested in determining how this change will affect the skill requirements of people in your team or how it may open up new work opportunities through shifting players and responsibilities. This change situation is illustrated in Figure 1-5.

Situation 2. Change Event Is Unknown/Impact is Known

This situation occurs when the effects of some unknown change event begin to show up in a variety of performance indicators and you are faced with the challenge of piecing this information together to form a "big-picture" view of the change event. Let's consider a brief example.

Assume that you hear that your organization is in the process of hiring a new director-level manager who will assume the newly created position of vice president of quality improvement (one of four vice presidential positions). Prior to the creation of this position, no separate quality improvement function existed in your department. You have also heard rumors that this manager had developed an excellent track record by establishing a quality-improvement program for one of your competitors and that the program had received rave reviews from one of your key customers. Finally, you have learned from a sales manager that a major customer has been putting pressure on your company and other suppliers to tighten up on the quality of their products. Putting the pieces of the puzzle together,

Figure 1-5. Change Event Situation 1.

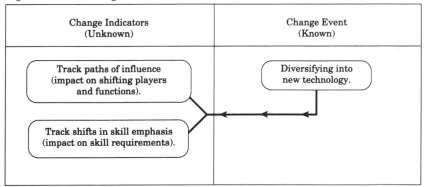

you decide that they add up to a major organizational push for quality improvement in response to both competitive pressure and changing customer requirements. This change situation is illustrated in Figure 1-6.

When attempting to complete the change analysis chart for this type of situation, begin by describing in the Your Observations area any change indicators that you've recently observed in your organization. Then continue adding to this information until you form a more complete picture of the change event.

To obtain additional value from the chart, follow these guidelines:

• Keep the chart where you can easily access it at work. Normally, information on large-scale changes comes in bits and pieces. If you don't make note of it, it's quickly forgotten in the hustle of the day.

• Give your completed chart to another manager or professional and ask that person to add comments. You can also use it as a springboard for dialoguing with other managers about anticipated change events.

• Use the chart as a planning tool whenever your manager asks you to evaluate the possible impact of an upcoming change and the steps that your department could take to prepare for this change. Similarly, you can use the chart as a team-building and planning activity with your team.

Figure 1-6.   Change Event Situation 2.

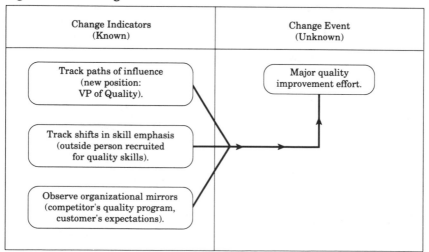

• Use the chart to help fill in missing information gaps. For example, assume you will soon be attending a departmental meeting where you will have the opportunity to ask questions on an upcoming organizational change. In this case, you could use the chart to identify gaps in your information about this change and to help you formulate questions to present during the meeting.

Empowerment Questionnaire

Suggested Guidelines

Perhaps you feel that a major roadblock to effective problem solving within your team is that members feel that they lack the authority, skills, and information they need to respond aggressively to problems. If this is the case, you might consider conducting an empowerment discussion with your team. Before engaging in such a discussion, consider the following six guidelines:

1. *Reduce the element of risk.* Team members frequently voice concerns that if they tell their managers that they feel micromanaged or impotent, they will be viewed as problem employees or complainers. To address such concerns, consider what actions you could take to encourage members to participate openly in an empowerment discussion. As a start, you could ask your company's training manager or organizational development specialist to serve as a third-party facilitator for this discussion or take the first few minutes of the discussion to formulate ground rules that encourage an open expression of views.

2. *Don't raise false expectations.* If it's impossible to give members additional freedom and autonomy over certain areas—if, for example, your manager has mandated that you retain direct control for a given area—be honest about it. Similarly, identify early in your discussion those areas in which you are unwilling to relinquish control.

3. *Be willing to "ante up."* In order to succeed, empowerment efforts typically require some type of initial "pump-priming" investment, for example, your commitment to taking the time to train members to perform a task.

4. *Remember that empowerment is an iterative process that occurs in stages.* If you feel that team members' requests for additional authority are unreasonable or excessive, brainstorm other options for addressing members' concerns. One useful technique is to draw a horizontal line

on a flipchart and indicate, on a scale of 1 to 7, the full range of empowerment for a given work area, with 1 representing complete team autonomy over a work area and 7 representing complete managerial control. Next, ask members how they would rate their current level of control over the area. Determine the range of agreement or disagreement on this point. Then work with your team to identify other options that lie between these two extreme points.

5. *Model the empowerment process through your approach to the discussion.* Empowerment is not something that you can do for your team. It's something that requires collaborative efforts with all members. Ask each member to describe his or her objectives for the meeting. Consider having an experienced member take the lead in facilitating the discussion, using the Questions for Discussion (presented later in this Tool Kit) as guidelines. During the discussion, try to let team members take the lead in presenting their views, and refrain from becoming overly directive or forcing your solutions on the team.

6. *At the end of the session, take the time to put together a detailed action plan.* By the end of your discussion with your team, each person should have a clear understanding of any new areas of accountability he or she has been given, the guidelines to follow when managing these areas of accountability, and the process your team will use to evaluate results and follow up on the success of empowerment activities.

How to Empower Your Team

There are many ways to increase the degree of control and autonomy your team members exert over their function. Empowerment actions include:

- Giving members more latitude to juggle assignments, resources, and work schedules
- Allowing members to interact directly with internal and external customers and suppliers or to represent the team when dealing with these individuals
- Providing a means for members to check or inspect their own work
- Working out a method by which members can track their own progress toward goals
- Obtaining members' input before recommending changes in facilities, methods, or capital equipment requests
- Enabling members to represent your team at meetings with other departments or senior managers

• Giving members additional authority to take immediate actions to prevent or resolve problems

Use this list to get members to consider the full range of empowerment issues in their discussion.

Questions for Discussion

Use the following questions as the basis for dialoguing with your team during your empowerment discussion:

1. What performance areas are being adversely affected because members lack the authority to make decisions or take action?
2. What types of problems are being created? What specific examples can we provide?
3. What would empowerment look like?
   • If team members were fully empowered within this area, what additional decisions would they be able to make?
   • What additional sign-off authority would they have?
   • To what additional information would they have access?
   • What actions could they take without prior approval and review by you, their manager?
4. What benefits would be obtained through this empowerment?
   • Fewer bottlenecks?
   • Better coverage on work?
   • Faster response to customers?
   • Less rework?
5. What additional risks would be involved?
   • Additional errors?
   • Resistance by other managers?
   • Temporary time lost while members learn to take over functions?
   • Greater coordination problems?
6. What steps could we take to minimize these risks?
   • Increase empowerment on an incremental basis?
   • Establish a trial period?
   • Use a peer-review process as a substitute for management review?
   • Provide additional training or mentoring to team members?
7. What first steps could we take to test out this increased empowerment?

8. How and when should we follow up on the results of these efforts?

Problem Scenario Exercise

Use this exercise to help your team identify potential problems on projects and to outline contingency plans for dealing with these problems. The exercise usually takes forty-five minutes to an hour to complete. To reduce the time requirement, consider asking members to perform steps 1 and 2 individually in advance (one member can be selected to collect all cards) and to complete the remaining steps as a team.

1. Define the performance area that you would like to review.
2. Have each member describe on three note cards up to three potential problems that might occur within this area. Members should focus on problems that require a quick response from your team.
3. Collect the cards and shuffle them, keeping them face down.
4. Ask the member on your left to pick a card, read it to the team, and answer the following questions:
   - What types of process indicators would help alert the team to the problem before it grows out of control?
   - What actions can be taken now to prevent the occurrence of the problem?
   - What factors need to be considered before the team takes corrective action to resolve the problem?
   - Based on an analysis of these factors, what corrective action is most appropriate?
5. Ask other members for their input, and record all ideas on the flipchart for later review. After all suggestions have been placed on the board, rank each suggestion in terms of its feasibility.
6. Continue discussion until you and your team can agree on the best means of establishing an early-warning system for the problem and guidelines for dealing with the problem.
7. Have the second team member in your group pull out a card and repeat Steps 4–7 until all problems are reviewed or until you run out of time.
8. Ask members to share their reactions to this exercise and their views regarding any areas of miscommunication that were cleared up through the exercise.

Figure 1-7.   The Communications Assessment Survey.

Communication Factors and Questions	Rating Scale
Trust	Never–Sometimes–Always
1. Do you feel that when communicating with you I'm honest and aboveboard?	1 .... 2 .... 3 .... 4 5
2. Are you willing to level with me without fear of criticism or reprisal?	1 .... 2 .... 3 .... 4 5
3. Do you believe that I keep confidences when privileged information is shared with me?	1 .... 2 .... 3 .... 4 5
Openness	
4. Do you feel that I hear you out completely before offering my point of view?	1 .... 2 .... 3 .... 4 5
5. Do you believe that I'm willing to listen openly to others' views when these views are different from my own?	1 .... 2 .... 3 .... 4 5
6. Do you feel that I'm willing to share my thoughts with you?	1 .... 2 .... 3 .... 4 5
Responsiveness	
7. Do you believe that I follow up on my promises?	1 .... 2 .... 3 .... 4 5
8. Do I present myself as someone who is caring and involved?	1 .... 2 .... 3 .... 4 5
9. Do you believe that I always do what I say I will do?	1 .... 2 .... 3 .... 4 5
Accessibility	
10. Are you able to get to me when you need me?	1 .... 2 .... 3 .... 4 5
11. Am I approachable? Do you feel comfortable walking into my office and starting a conversation?	1 .... 2 .... 3 .... 4 5
12. Do I set aside enough time each week to meet with our team?	1 .... 2 .... 3 .... 4 5

Improvement Suggestions

13. What is one thing that I could personally do to support better communication within our team? ....
....

14. What is one change that you would like to see made in the way that the members of our team interact with each other? ....

15. Can you describe a type of situation in which information has been held up or problems have grown out of control because of poor team communication? What suggestions do you have for dealing with these problems? ....
....
....
....

This exercise will not only help your team establish early-warning systems for dealing with fast-breaking problems but will also develop members' skills by encouraging them to analyze problems carefully (do they consider all factors before suggesting a course of action?) and to develop innovative solutions to problems (do they offer only the most obvious and pat solutions, or do they engage in creative problem solving?). Finally, it will show you whether members are erroneously assuming that they lack the authority or expertise needed to handle certain problem situations.

Communications Assessment Survey

Use the Communications Assessment Survey (Figure 1-7) to discover how your team members view your communication style. You will usually obtain more complete and honest feedback if you give respondents the option of remaining anonymous and if all survey responses are collected and averaged by a member of the team.

Notes

1. Interview with Patrick Miller, director of human resources for TECO Transport and Trade, May 27, 1993.
2. Sheila M. Eby, "PSSSST! Do You Want to Know a Secret?" *Inc.*, in *Guide to Small Business Success* (1987). Reprinted with permission, *Inc.* magazine. Copyright 1987 Goldhirsh Group, Inc., 38 Commercial Wharf, Boston, MA 02110.
3. Interview with Joe Ferrel, senior planning analyst for Florida Power and Light, April 1993.
4. Interview with Mark Johnson, manager of quality curriculum for AT&T Paradyne, April 1993.
5. Interview with Joe Dunsmore, senior marketing manager for AT&T Paradyne, May 1993.
6. Interview with Brian Chitester, director of process improvement for Pepsi Cola, June 1993.

Challenge 2

Banish Bedlam
And Burnout

The Rising Stress Curve

When organizations encounter tough times, performance standards rise, resources are strictly rationed, and jobs become less secure. As a result, the working environment becomes more stressful, and burnout emerges as a serious performance problem. In addition, during tough times many managers make the mistake of reducing communication with their teams, leaving employees feeling isolated and fearful about the unknown. Given these work conditions, it's easy to understand why employees experience higher levels of stress and anxiety during difficult times. Research studies by organizations such as the Northwestern National Life Insurance Company (NWNL)[1] and Right Associates have shown that work stress has become a detrimental factor for many organizations.[2]

Whenever I talk about the importance of managing work stress, I inevitably encounter a certain amount of cynicism from managers who argue that a high level of stress actually contributes to good performance by raising employee's energy levels and enthusiasm. They suggest that the only thing stress management programs accomplish is to turn high-productivity work environments into relaxed and unproductive Shangri-las.

This is a silly argument at best. Stress is a sign that excessive wear and tear are being placed on a system. While a moderate amount of stress is necessary for good performance, excessive stress does not indicate that a team is performing at its best. It merely strips a team of energy that could be more productively directed elsewhere as team members seek ways to buffer themselves against the adverse effects of stress. Like the Starship Enterprise after it has been hit by a blast of photon torpedoes, stressed-out members tend to shut down everything but essential life-support systems.

To understand the relationship that exists between work stress and performance, picture someone racing a car across the Utah salt flats on the hottest day of the year, saying, "Look at the temperature climb in my engine! Now I'm really getting good performance!" Now picture that person intentionally puncturing his radiator to produce an even greater increase in the car's engine temperature. Sounds pretty silly, doesn't it? Equally silly is the manager who says, "I'm really getting performance out of my group now; just look at them sweat!" Once again, excessive stress is a sign of poorly displaced energy. Teams attempting to survive tough times need to apply their energy in the most effective way possible.

Your Role as Stress Buffer

At this point you may be thinking, "Okay, even assuming that excessive stress does lead to poor performance, what am I expected to do about it? I'm not a trained psychologist or therapist." That's right, but, unfortunately, you are stuck with this situation. You depend on your team to meet your objectives, and you can't afford to wait until your organization becomes less stressful. Like it or not, you play a pivotal role in helping your team successfully cope with work stress.

Since the early 1970s, abundant research has shown that one of the most critical factors for coping successfully with stress is the presence of a solid support system—those networks of interpersonal relationships that, during periods of stress and trauma, provide emotional and social support and assistance. Support systems offer a sense that one isn't alone with one's problems, that there is someone out there who is willing to help. Research has shown that when people are exposed to severe stresses, such as illness or the death of a spouse, those who have good support systems are much less likely to suffer from heart problems and other major stress disorders.[3] Additional research has shown that the most effective buffer against work stress is not one's friends, coworkers, or spouse but one's manager.[4] The actions you as manager take and the relationships you form with your team members thus directly influence their ability to cope with work stress.

Although in these times it's almost impossible to eliminate work stress, the strategies in this chapter will introduce you to several actions you can take to help your team maintain its performance in high-stress work environments.

Warning Symptoms

It's not difficult to tell when your team is suffering from stress over-load. Just look for the following symptoms and check any that may apply:

❑ *Increased conflicts.* Team members engage in petty bickering or flare-ups over conflicts that in the past would have been easily resolved, and meet performance challenges with finger-pointing and blaming, rather than productive problem solving.

❑ *Reduced effort.* Members may withdraw physically or emotion-ally from team projects or be reluctant to provide other team members with needed support, or to volunteer for "extra effort" projects, such as presentations to senior managers.

❑ *Health problems.* Members appear totally exhausted two hours into the day. Other health symptoms are a high level of fatigue, a sharp rise in absenteeism, and an increase in safety problems.

❑ *Sense of being overwhelmed.* Members immediately react to any announced changes or assignments with a great deal of resis-tance and anxiety. Any impending change is viewed by your group as a harbinger of bad news.

❑ *Poor two-way communication.* The last symptom, poor two-way communication, is so important that I want to deal with it sepa-rately. While some managers of stressed-out teams experience a sharp increase in the number of complaints from members, a far more serious warning symptom is when your group suddenly stops communicating with you. Do any of the following situa-tions sound familiar?

- Are members reluctant to bring you bad news? Do they inten-tionally hide their own or other members' work problems from you?
- Have you ever overheard members complaining about work problems, only to have them immediately cease all conversa-tion when you enter the room?
- Have you found that members purposely avoid you or no longer invite you to eat lunch with them?
- Have you been intentionally excluded from joining in after-work social functions?
- Do members seem particularly anxious or upset whenever they communicate with you?

- Do members draw a sharp line between "you" (you and all senior-level managers) and "us"?
- Do members go out of their way to ask each other for help, rather than approach you for advice and information?
- Do members seem to mistrust the information you present?
- If your team has recently conducted an anonymous manager-feedback survey on your leadership, do the results seem very out of sync with the face-to-face feedback you are receiving from your team?

If these situations sound familiar, they should serve as warnings that team members are attempting to cope with stress by erecting barriers between you and them. The problem is that the lack of two-way communication leads to a number of secondary problems, which produce even more stress for you and your team.

Strategies

During your years as a manager, you've developed a leadership style that is by now deeply ingrained. While changing your overall leadership style might prove very difficult, a more reasonable strategy is to look for ways to modify aspects of your leadership behavior that may be contributing to the stress of your team, such as the manner in which you respond to members' concerns or your approach when making job assignments.

A second strategy involves implementing changes that can decrease the stress level in your workplace. Such changes might include looking for ways to expand members' range of control over their work, ensuring that members have periods of concentrated effort, encouraging your team to focus on the controllable aspects of stressful change, using humor in the workplace, and teaching members coping skills for dealing with some of the most frequently encountered work stressors.

Strategy 1. Adjust Your Leadership Behavior

- **Don't create needless stress.** Avoid adding needless stress to an already stressed-out team. Some of the leadership behaviors that tend to trigger work stress are listed on the next page. Note any of those behaviors that pertain to your performance. In addition, because most people are not accurate observers of their own behavior, consider using this checklist to ask for feedback on your leadership style from a trusted team member or work associate. Do you:

- Vacillate on decisions, procrastinate on decisions, or rush into decisions without first having sufficient information?
- Create arbitrary deadlines for projects? That is, do your deadlines take into account real job requirements?
- Generate conflicts by encouraging win-lose competition among members?
- Criticize members in public rather than in private?
- Make comments that make people feel threatened about the loss of their jobs?
- Intentionally withhold information from members?
- Pit people against each other?
- Use force and threats to win discussions with members?
- Gossip about members behind their backs?
- Withdraw your support, assistance, and energy from your group?
- Create conflicts between your team and others and then thrust your members into the middle of these problems?
- Become loud and vocally abusive whenever you discover a work problem?

- **Monitor your stress level.** Don't use your team as an outlet for your own stress. If you find yourself ready to climb the walls because of something your boss or your supplier did, avoid taking your frustration out on your team. Instead, before interacting with your team, give yourself time to recover, and carefully think through the following questions:

- How much of what I'm upset about is directly within the control of my team?
- Are they really the target of my anger?
- Am I angry with my team or just anxious about my job?
- If I blow up, am I really going to move the job along faster, or will I simply create more problems?
- Do team members really understand the full context of my anger and frustration? If they don't seem to understand the significance of a problem, is it because part of the situation is outside of their visibility?

- **Keep things in perspective.** When people become anxious and stressed out, they tend to view all irritations and problems as critical. If you become emotionally drained over small, inconsequential problems, you will deplete energy resources that would normally be re-

served for dealing with critical challenges. In this respect, you will perform like a marathon racer who exhausts herself by running a series of
high-speed sprints before the race is even under way. To conserve your
energy, learn to keep your problems in perspective by identifying
those few work situations that truly require a high level of vigilance
and effort. The Work Problem Tracking Chart in the Tool Kit may be
helpful in keeping your problems in perspective.

• **Make decisions during low-stress periods.** Although it's impossible to predict with 100 percent certainty the types of situations
that will trigger excessive stress, if you carefully track your stress over
a period of days or weeks you will probably find that you experience
a stress cycle of predictable highs and lows. For example, your stress
level may build immediately before you are to meet with your manager or certain customers. Highlight on your weekly calendar any upcoming events or responsibilities that are likely to create stress for you.
If possible, avoid making key decisions during these periods, and save
important decision-making meetings for times when your stress level
is moderate and your attention is fully focused on the task at hand. Be
ruthlessly honest with yourself about recognizing situations in which
you are not emotionally and mentally prepared to wrestle with difficult work issues.

• **Regulate your level of work direction.** Managers experiencing
excessive stress tend to have difficulty balancing the degree of supervision they provide to their groups. Some managers intervene too
quickly, resulting in micromanagement and nervous hovering. Others
go to the opposite extreme, procrastinating about acting on stressful
work situations until their stress level builds up to the point where
they overwhelm their group with critical feedback on a variety of problems. Ask yourself the following questions to determine the best time
to confront your members about performance problems:

• How important is this project in the overall context of things?
• Can I separate my own personal frustrations from the management needs of this project? Do members already understand
  what went wrong? Are they working on a correction? What do
  I want to accomplish with my intervention?
• If I were one of the team members, when would I need to receive
  feedback on this project? When is the most appropriate time to
  speak with members so that they can begin to take corrective
  action?
• What is the trend line for this work area? Is performance gradually, consistently declining, or is it rapidly degenerating? Is per-

formance generally good except for periodic, erratic problem points? If I do nothing for the next few days, what risks do I run?

- When was the last time I spoke with the team about this work problem? What advice or suggestions did I give? Have I provided enough time for members to demonstrate a performance improvement?

One way to make sure that you provide an adequate amount of supervision is to use project schedule charts. You can develop these charts with your team prior to implementing any project and list ahead of time two types of interventions: (1) the dates on which you and your members will meet to conduct routine status reviews on the project, and (2) the types of performance problems that, should they occur, need to be brought to your attention immediately. Have the project schedule posted on a wall by your team's work area so that you can quickly glance at it if you feel the need to make an unscheduled progress check. The Project Milestone Chart provided in the Tool Kit for Challenge 1 may serve as a good model.

- **Resist the tendency to tighten up.** I'm sure that your manager has already given you a speech about the need for maintaining tight control over your team until your organization gets back on track. This sounds great, but the question is, control over what? Do you really need to inventory the number of paper clips or pencils used by your group each month?

To manage work stress, use the techniques presented in Challenge 3 to pinpoint your team's most important responsibilities. Once you've done this, you can concentrate on managing those responsibilities that are essential to your team's survival and that represent high-risk performance areas. Again, the Work Problem Tracking Chart in this chapter's Tool Kit will be useful in determining the risk levels associated with different types of decisions and actions.

- **Provide clear communications.** Fight the urge to withdraw from your team and stay in your office. You are your team's "door of visibility" to the rest of your organization. If the door is closed, your team will feel that it has been locked in the mushroom cellar without access to needed information or direction.

Share any and all information you have on important changes now occurring in your company. Be honest about what is fact and what is rumor. Consider having selected team members accompany you to departmental meetings so that they can form their own opinions about impending changes.

In addition, be careful about playing favorites. If your team is experiencing stress, it becomes very important to balance your communications and to make an effort to reach everyone. Make it a point to eat lunch with a different team member every day and to talk with members individually to find out about the status of their work. If time is a problem, use other techniques such as PC networking, electronic mail systems, or a note board in a designated area of your office to keep members on track regarding new information that can affect them. Challenge 1 provides a number of options for enhancing communication links with your team.

• **Listen fully to members' concerns.** As Patrick Miller, director of human resources for TECO Transport and Trade, suggests, listening is a key tactic to help members manage stress: "Listening becomes critical; you need to hear the emotional messages which lie between the literal messages and give people a chance to share their fears and concerns. In addition, you need to be perceived by members as honestly offering help without pushing help."[5]

Allow members an opportunity to air their fears and concerns openly. When members begin to voice their anger and frustration, resist the tendency to respond immediately by justifying your company's actions or telling them that you agree with their views. Just listen, and acknowledge that you understand their concerns. Communicate that you want to work with team members to make certain that they perform at their best during these tough times. Keep in mind that no one is expecting you to perform as a therapist or counselor during these discussions. You don't necessarily have to have answers to everyone's problems. The important thing is that you position yourself as someone who is open, interested, and concerned for your team's welfare.

If you are experiencing stress yourself, you may find it hard to listen to members because your attention level will continually wander to other subjects. You can correct this problem by restricting your standard open-door policy, instead setting aside times in which you are able to give members your full attention. Also, ask members to avoid engaging you in hit-and-run conversations in the hallways. If you feel that it will be impossible to enforce this rule, keep a pad with you at all times to take notes (no matter how simple the discussion) on what is said and on required follow-up actions.

Before meeting with a member who wishes to air concerns:

• Clear your desk of any projects that could distract you from the discussion.

- Ask other members not to barge in on you unless there is an emergency.
- Have someone cover calls for you to avoid additional distractions.
- Provide a clear mental focus point for the discussion by summarizing during the first few minutes of the discussion (1) the team member's key purpose for talking with you, (2) the type of help or assistance that the member is requesting from you, and (3) how long the discussion will last.
- Take notes during, not after, the discussion. If you have a computer, create a *Team Concerns File*, and enter notes directly into this file during the discussion. This will eliminate wasting time later on searching for notes and will provide a single focal point for referencing team concerns.
- If, during the discussion, your attention wanders to other important subjects, ask the speaker to stop for a second while you make a quick memory-jogger note for later reference. If you find yourself unable to concentrate on the subject at hand, honestly explain that you are having trouble focusing on the discussion and reschedule the discussion for a later time. Avoid one of the most common mistakes made by stressed-out managers—trying to be two places at once.

• **Adjust the pressure valve.** Chances are there are a few team members on whom you rely for support. When work pressure builds, you may tend to put a lot more pressure on these individuals because you know that they are reliable and will put in extra effort. The problem is that if you aren't careful, you will both quickly burn out your star performers and send a message to the rest of the team that poor performance is rewarded with less work. If you discover that some team members are walking out the door each day at quitting time while others are pulling two or three hours of overtime, something is wrong. Talk to members to find out whether the problem involves an unbalanced workload or a performance problem; then act accordingly.

One way of balancing your team's workload is through weekly meetings. Ask members to outline their assignments, estimate time commitments for the upcoming week, and suggest ways of reallocating assignments to provide for the fairest possible distribution of work. If members put in a lot of overtime, consider giving them compensatory time off to recover their energy. The Team Transition Chart in the Tool Kit for Challenge 5 is an effective tool for balancing workloads among members.

- **Be a strong advocate.** An important tactic for managing stress is to be a strong advocate in representing your team's concerns to senior managers or other groups. You might also ask your manager to meet briefly with team members to provide them with a broader picture of the changes now under way at your company. In Challenge 6, on forging alliances, we provide suggestions on how to be a team advocate.

- **Remain flexible regarding different work styles.** Still another important factor in managing team stress is the ability to respond flexibly to the different work styles of your members. A good example of this is presented by Cindy Durning, director of human resources for Times Publishing Company:

> It's important to identify the working styles of your staff and proceed accordingly. I work with a person who is very detail-oriented and not very concept-oriented. I found that when presenting a project to this person I had a tendency to become impatient. I resolved this by taking him out to lunch and then placing him in a situation in which he was under less pressure to discuss the project. I find that people who are detail-oriented feel the need to grasp things more clearly before they begin to tackle them and are sometimes afraid to raise questions at work. On the other hand, another member of my team is very bottom-line oriented. With this individual, I can breeze in, ask a few questions, and breeze out. There isn't the same need for detail.[6]

Strategy 2: Create a Stress-Managed Environment

- **Provide periods of concentrated effort.** During high-stress periods people usually find it more difficult to concentrate on the work in front of them. These are the times that phones ring off the hook and people find themselves overrun by walk-in visitors. One technique for creating a stress-managed environment is to meet with your team to determine the most quiet, uninterrupted location in your facility. This might be an unused conference room, the company cafeteria (morning or late afternoon), or even an isolated corner of your office. In addition, see if your group is willing to set up a schedule which will enable members to cover each others' phones and handle walk-in interruptions. The goal should be to provide each member with one to two hours of uninterrupted, concentrated effort each day. This will enable them to follow through on difficult projects, concentrate more effectively on their work, and have a re-energizing period during the day.

• **Focus on the controllables.** One of the biggest factors in work stress is the fear of being overwhelmed by factors outside one's control. For your group, this means dealing with large-scale changes that are perceived as unknown, uncontrollable, and potentially dangerous. Look for ways to keep your group apprised of important changes and redirect its focus to those aspects of change that are within its control. Challenge 1 provides a number of useful suggestions for managing change.

• **Use humor in the workplace.** One of the most effective techniques for dealing with stress is to use your sense of humor to keep problems in perspective and to elevate people when they are feeling depressed. In the process of writing this book, I spoke with many human resources and line managers who said that maintaining a sense of humor was the key tactic used by managers in their organizations who were able to deal successfully with stress.

Mark Johnson, manager of quality curriculum for AT&T Paradyne, says that humor—the ability to laugh at normally distressing or challenging work situations—is especially important to job survival. Some of the managers in his company use the following stress management technique:

> We took carefully selected cartoons . . . and removed the captions, then had a contest to see the funniest sayings that employees could come up with. An example would be a cartoon showing a soldier riding back from battle with fifteen arrows stuck in his back. Many people came up with some really off-the-wall comments, but we were careful not to censor them. People found the comments hilarious and stress-reducing.[7]

Cindy Durning, director of human resources for Times Publishing Company, uses the following tactic:

> We are in a high-stress, burnout field. We often don't hear about something unless there's a problem. Often people will call us with a lot of crazy complaints. As a stress reliever we perform a lot of impromptu miniskits focusing on people who call us about the craziest things, or we share with each other some of the most unrealistic questions of the week. The important thing is that we use this as a stress reliever for our own team, and we poke fun at these things

only when we are by ourselves, never when we are with other departments.[8]

Another one of our clients mentioned that her department has an informal yearly celebration during which they hand out a lot of crazy awards. One of these is the annual Mylanta award, given to the person whose project created the most heartburn.

Humor can help insulate your team from even the most traumatic work challenge—downsizing. An excellent example was shared with me by Bevan Gray, organizational development consultant for John Allen Life Insurance. Several years ago, Bevan worked with Allied Stores, which suffered a major downsizing when it was purchased by another company. To help keep morale up during the downsizing process and to provide employees and managers with a sense of camaraderie, Bevan and several other managers decided to invite all employees to a "pink slip party."

Party invitations were given out as pink slips, and employees were asked to dress in pink (for pink slips) and black (for mourning). The vice president of personnel was given a crown and honored as Miss Pink Slip (she had to make some of the difficult termination arrangements and then was herself one of the first people terminated). In addition, office jokes about the situation were encouraged: "What are they going to do about it, fire us?" Pink achievement awards were given out to selected employees to affirm that, despite the downsizings, their performance was appreciated.

The purpose of all of this tongue-in-cheek humor was to laugh in the face of adversity. As Bevan says, "We created an environment that said that humor was okay and that humor was what was going to get us through this thing."[9]

• **Expand your team's range of control.** A significant amount of stress research shows that the more control people exert over difficult work situations, the more they are able to cope with those situations. In the work environment, you can help regulate stress by looking for ways to place control in the hands of your team. For example, in the NWNL study, researchers found that managers can alleviate stress among employees by giving employees more discretion to negotiate deadlines, manage their own work loads, and control other aspects of their work.[10] How about your team? In what small ways could you increase your team members' level of control over their work stressors? Meet with your team and ask members to help you list ways to expand their range of control over their work areas.

I recognize that most readers are probably finding themselves caught between the desire to provide their members with additional control and autonomy and the concern that such additional control will lead to needless performance risks and censure by senior management. The Empowerment Questionnaire provided in Chapter 1's Tool Kit can help you balance the elements of increased team empowerment and risk.

• **Teach coping skills.** You can use the Stress Situations Guide found in this chapter's Tool Kit to teach members how to perform at their best when facing the most frequently encountered high-stress work situations. Another way to implement this tactic is to provide members with books and guides, such as my book *Lifeboat Strategies: How to Keep Your Career Above Water During Tough Times—or Any Time* (New York: AMACOM, 1994), which provide suggestions and guidelines for self-managing stress. An additional approach might involve looking for low-cost stress management workshops that members can take after hours or on weekends through local adult education programs, colleges, or community mental health agencies.

• **Periodically audit stress factors in your environment.** Conduct an audit to identify factors that may be creating stress for your team. This doesn't have to be a tedious or expensive process. The Tool Kit provides information on how to obtain a copy of the NWNL Workplace Stress Test, available through the Northwestern National Life Insurance Company.

TOOL KIT

NWNL Workplace Stress Test

The following information was adapted with permission from the NWNL study on employee burnout.[11]

The NWNL Workplace Stress Test was developed by Northwestern National Life Insurance Company in 1991 as part of a two-year research study on work stress. In 1992 the NWNL developed a revised version of the test that allows companies to compare their stress scores with those from other organizations. The test consists of forty-six statements covering six major areas:

1. Employee support and training
2. Work conditions

3. Organizational change
4. Employee benefits
5. Progressive programs
6. Job design and physical environment

Respondents are asked to indicate their degree of agreement with each statement on a five-degree scale. Their scoring profiles provide valuable information on factors that may be contributing to work stress.

NWNL makes available to interested employers, at no cost, a test packet that includes directions for administering the test, a sample letter that can be presented to employees, the test itself, a scoring key, tally sheets, and a scoring guide. It should be noted that NWNL grants permission only to employers to copy the NWNL Workplace Stress Test for distribution to employees within their organizations. NWNL also has available two copyrighted research reports. NWNL does not permit individuals or stress management organizations to copy these studies and does not make multiple copies of the reports available for distribution to stress management organizations' clients or other external audiences. All requests for the test should be directed to Northwestern National Life, P.O. Box 20, Route 6528, Minneapolis, Minn. 55440.

Work Problem Tracking Chart

It's easier to deal with work stressors if you can place them in perspective and remind yourself that they don't represent insurmountable problems. Unfortunately, many times people attempt to manage stress by keeping problems at a mental distance and putting them out of their thoughts. The difficulty is that the problems tend to creep back in when least expected, hovering on the periphery of awareness like some dangerous and amorphous dark cloud. To put work stressors into context it is necessary to focus attention directly on them. Like the monsters of childhood, work stressors tend to dissipate when brought into the light.

To focus light on your work stressors, follow these steps to complete the Work Problem Tracking Chart. A model chart is provided in Figure 2-1.

1. *Work Problems.* List all the work situations that are currently creating stress in your life. These may include technical and people

Figure 2-1. The Work Problem Tracking Chart Model.

Work Problems	Worst Possible Scenario	I/W	P/W	Best Possible Scenario	I/B	P/B	Stress
We are being threatened with additional budget cutbacks.	Our budget is cut in half and I lose 3 people from my group.	7	3	I can convince our general manager to restrict budget reductions to 10% and to allow me to wait until the end of the year before considering staff reductions.	5	4	6
We aren't able to resolve our problems with XYZ.	We lose the account, putting additional pressure on us to reduce costs.	5	2	We not only salvage the account but generate an excellent response from XYZ and increase our sales.	7	6	4
Continued conflicts with JB over the allocation of sales staff.	The problem escalates, dividing the team and making us both look bad in the eyes of our managers.	4	3	We resolve the problem quickly and establish a good work relationship.	5	5	3

problems that need to be resolved, projects that are giving you trouble, or conditions to which you are having difficulty adjusting (working overtime, excessive noise). Continue on a blank page if you need more room. At this stage, don't be concerned that you are including minor problems. If your energy and attention are being diverted to them, they aren't minor. My only caveat here is to be specific. Instead of writing, "A problem with other groups," you might write, "The schedule delays I'm encountering from Bill in the finance department."

2. *Worst Possible Scenario.* List your fears regarding the worst possible outcomes that could occur if these problems aren't resolved. Again, don't censor yourself. If you feel that failing to meet a schedule deadline would lead to a bad performance review, write this down. After you have finished writing, ask yourself the question, "What would happen then?" If, for example, you believe that a bad performance review would result in a job termination, write this down. The point of this step is to look objectively at how you may be leading yourself down a path of negative, self-sabotaging thoughts. When you see how you are mentally connecting all the possible events in your scenario, it becomes much easier for you to spot negative and erroneous thinking.

3. *Impact of Worst Scenario (IW).* Use a 1–7 scale to rate the potential impact of the worst scenario that you've created, with a score of 7 representing the most potentially serious outcome (death).

4. *Probability of Worst Scenario (P/W).* Rate on a 1–7 scale the likelihood that your worst scenario will occur, with a score of 7 representing a probability close to 100 percent.

5. *Best Possible Scenario.* List the best possible outcome you could expect if this situation is resolved as you would like it to be. The purpose of this step is to keep yourself focused on not only the potential dangers but also the possible payoffs that can lead from difficult work situations.

6. *Impact of Best Scenario (I/B).* Use a 1–7 scale to rate the potential impact of the best possible scenario that you've created, with a score of 7 representing the best possible outcome.

7. *Probability of Best Scenario (P/B).* Rate on a 1–7 scale the likelihood that your best possible scenario will occur, with a score of 7 representing a probability which is close to 100 percent.

8. *Overall Stress Level.* You've now created a breakdown of possible outcomes ranging from good to bad for each work problem you've listed, along with a rough assessment of the relative impact and likeli-

hood of occurrence of each. Use this information to form an overall opinion of the stress represented by each of these situations. Then, in this column, rank each problem from least to most important, with a rank of 1 representing the situation you are least concerned about. If you have a problem determining the relative ranking of any two problems, consider the degree of urgency of each. Give the lower ranking to the situation that is least urgent.

9. After you've ranked your work problems, describe each problem in a single sentence, and write your descriptions on paper to keep at your work station for weekly review. Whenever you find your attention drifting among different concerns, use this list as an anchor to refocus your attention on your most important work problems. As you make progress on each problem, cross it off your list. Consider sharing the list with a trusted associate or friend to gain some additional objectivity on each problem you've listed. Update the list once each week or as needed.

Stress Situations Guide

This guide may prove helpful when you or any of your team members are attempting to cope with either of the following stressors.

Situation 1: Managing Conflicts

1. *Quarantine them.* Whenever possible, quarantine conflicts by keeping additional issues out of the discussion. Anyone who has ever observed arguments knows that in most conflicts there is a tendency to drag in the kitchen sink. Unfortunately, once the scope of the conflict has been enlarged, the conflict is much more difficult to resolve. Before beginning a conflict discussion with another associate, write a one- or two-sentence description of how you view the conflict and then ask a friend to review this description to make certain it doesn't contain any blame casting or personal attacks. If it does, reword it so that it represents an objective opening for discussion and is focused on a single issue for review.

2. *Enter with a written agenda.* Bring a written description with you to the discussion, along with the main points that you would like to cover. When you begin, read your description and ask the other party if it provides a fair and objective summary of the conflict. If she disagrees, take the time to reword it until it represents both of your views.

Next, ask that the discussion be limited to this topic so that the two of you can reach closure on this issue during the meeting. Don't proceed with the discussion until you've accomplished this. In addition, keep your list in front of you to prevent the discussion from going off-track.

3. *Avoid personal attacks.* During the discussion, avoid engaging in personal attacks or taking cheap shots at the other person. To do this, prior to the discussion practice presenting some of the main points you would like to get across to the other person. Make an audiotape of this practice session, and screen it for any comments that sound overly critical or personal. During your discussion, if the other party engages in personal comments, try to filter out these comments and focus back on the issue at hand. For example:

Other: The problem is your lack of responsibility in this area. You promise one schedule date and then deliver another.

You: So from your point of view, a key issue is that you need to know that I will keep my commitments on schedules, right?

4. *Take the wind out of the other person's sails.* People often enter into conflict discussions pumped up with a high degree of anger, a defense mechanism against anticipated hostility from the other party.

To defuse hostility, send messages that will calm the other person and take the wind out of his sails. Offer the option of meeting in his office or at your work area. Avoid meeting in a public work area, because people are more likely to become ego-involved in conflicts when their peers or subordinates can overhear (ever watch children daring each other to fight in a playground?). Select a time when neither of you will feel rushed or pressured.

During the discussion, avoid standing or leaning over the other person. Sit in a comfortable position, and try to relax your face and breathing. Avoid talking in a rushed or clipped manner. Offer the other person some coffee. Before responding, say to the other person, "Obviously you have a lot of strong feelings about this. Before we go on, I want to make sure that I understand you correctly." Often, at this point, the other party will quickly throw out a few angry points and then brace himself (you can see this in a tightening of the face and muscles) for your attack. Once again, take the wind out of his sails by summarizing what you've heard and then encouraging him to continue. Then briefly summarize the speaker's key points.

5. *Place disagreements within the context of agreement.* During conflicts, people tend to focus on those areas on which they disagree with-

out fully considering areas of agreement. Before commenting on any disagreement, quickly list those points on which you and your partner agree, then lead into your area of disagreement. Say something like "I feel that we are in agreement on several points," and then list them and say, "The one area where we seem to disagree is. . . . You seem to feel . . . whereas I believe that. . . . Is that the way you see things?"

Situation 2: Responding to Criticism

1. *Put the person and situation in perspective.* When people are under stress it's easy for them to blow out of proportion any critical feedback that's presented. If you find yourself criticized, remind yourself that the criticism addresses only one aspect of your performance and that there are many other areas in which your performance excels. If someone directs a general criticism at you, help that person focus in on more specific feedback. For example:

Other: You've really got to improve the way you are managing your relationships with your customers.

You: When you say "not managing relationships effectively," what exactly do you mean? Do you feel I'm being rude to customers? Are we talking about my entire customer base?

Other: No, you seem to be well liked by your customers, and things appear to be okay with your established customers. However, a couple of times I've felt that you've made promises to entice new customers that I don't feel you can possibly meet. For example, I couldn't help overhearing your conversation with ABC Corporation the other day on the phone, and I noticed that. . . ."

2. *Remember that you are not the target.* If someone makes personal comments about you or criticizes you too strongly, keep in mind that stressed-out people tend to indiscriminately dump on other people. Remind yourself, "I am not the target. I just happened to be in the way when this person decided to dump on me. It's her problem, not mine."

3. *Turn criticisms into desired aims.* Criticism often takes the form of telling people what we don't want them to do. Unfortunately, in this sense it provides little informational value because it doesn't spell out what desired behavior looks like. Whenever you receive negative feedback, ask the other person to clarify her expectations of you. If needed, provide some suggestions. For example:

Other: That budget forecast was really a surprise. When I took it into the directors' meeting I ended up with egg all over my face. The actuals were completely out of line with your original projections. I want to make certain this doesn't happen again.

You: Well, as you know, given the number of project readjustments we've been having, it's almost impossible to provide an accurate, annual budget projection. Are you saying you expect me to increase the accuracy of our projections?

Other: I realize you can't do that, but I would appreciate being forewarned the next time around so that I can give our director more advance warning of any increases prior to the annual budget review.

You: So you want me to generate a quarterly budget projection?

Other: It doesn't even have to be that formal. Just pull your budget trend line out of your spreadsheet package and fax it to me for review with warning flags on those areas that are beginning to run over and a handwritten note as to why. Also, I'd really like to receive that on a monthly, not a quarterly, basis.

4. *Get agreement on what you've done right.* When under stress, people often become overly sensitive to criticism and convince themselves that there is little they are doing effectively. To obtain a big-picture view of criticism, ask the other party to share with you things she likes about your performance; then discuss the criticism within the context of your overall performance. For example:

You: So if I understand you, you're saying that you like the way I'm managing the bid process, that my documentation is complete and accurate, and that I could do even better if I worked on providing a more timely response to bids. Is that about it?

Notes

1. Northwestern National Life Insurance Company (NWNL), "Employee Burnout: America's Newest Epidemic" (Minneapolis, Minn.: NWNL, 1991); NWNL, "Employee Burnout: Causes and Cures, Part 1, Employee Stress Levels" (Minneapolis, Minn.: NWNL, 1992).
2. *Lessons Learned: Dispelling the Myths of Downsizing,* 2d ed. (Philadelphia: Right Management Consulting, 1992).
3. D. C. Glass and Jerome Singer, *Urban Stress: Experiments on Noise and Social Stressors* (New York: Academic Press, 1972); I. L. Janis,

Psychological Stress (New York: Wiley, 1958); Alan A. McLean, *Work Stress*, (Reading, Mass.: Addison-Wesley, 1979).

4. S. G. Haynes, E. D. Eaker, and M. Feinleib, "The Effect of Employment, Family, and Job Stress on Coronary Heart Disease Pattern in Women," in E. B. Gold, ed., *The Changing Risk of Disease in Women: An Epidemiological Approach* (Lexington, Mass.: The Collanne Press), pp. 37–48; McLean, *Work Stress*.

5. Interview with Patrick Miller, director of human resources at TECO Transport and Trade, May 17, 1993.

6. Interview with Cindy Durning, director of human resources for Times Publishing Company, March 1993.

7. Interview with Mark Johnson, manager of quality curriculum for AT&T Paradyne, April 1993.

8. Interview with Cindy Durning

9. Interview with Bevan Gray, organizational development consultant for John Allen Life Insurance, 1992.

10. NWNL, "Employee Burnout."

11. Northwestern National Life Insurance Company (NWNL), "Employee Burnout: Causes and Cures, Part 2, Addressing Stress in your Organization" (Minneapolis, Minn.: NWNL, 1992).

Challenge 3

Focus Efforts

Combating the Activity Trap and Performance Myopia

How do you deal with a heavy workload? If your in-basket is over-flowing and you are frantically trying to keep pace with your assignments, you know how difficult it is to sort quickly through conflicting priorities and gauge the relative importance of your team's various activities.

As you attempt to focus your team's efforts, you will probably fall into the activity trap—the tendency to evaluate performance by the amount of effort invested in an activity, rather than by the results. During tough times the activity trap can become a serious problem, as you get caught up in day-to-day firefighting and find it difficult to step back and take an objective look at your team's performance.

Another stumbling block is performance myopia—the failure to look outside yourself to see your performance through the eyes of your customers. Performance myopia is most likely to occur within highly specialized and insular functions that thrive inside large, rigidly structured organizations. When people suffer from performance myopia, they tend to place very well-defined boundaries around their responsibilities. They develop their own languages and rituals (policies and procedures) that, although perfectly understandable to others in their group, are bewildering to the group's internal and external customers. Once the group completes its work, the result is thrown over the wall to the group's customers, who struggle with it as best they can.

The key destructive element in performance myopia is the failure to carefully evaluate how one's work is used by others: Does it help or hinder customers' efforts, and can it be improved upon to support organizational goals? In fact, workers in many departments view the idea of sitting down and talking with customers as meeting with the enemy. Information is jealously guarded, and tight control is maintained over processes and procedures. The following example shows how this nearsightedness can damage both a team's performance and its reputation.

After completing a purchase order, line managers in an aerospace company often had to wait several weeks for a response from their suppliers, only to find that the purchase order had been returned along with a cryptic note from the company's purchasing agents stating that the order "doesn't comply with correct purchase order procedures." In some cases, such bottlenecks resulted in serious delays in the shipment of critical parts.

When one company program manager asked the purchasing department for assistance in correcting her purchase orders, she was told that as a manager she was supposed to know these procedures and that the purchasing department couldn't take the time to train her. The purchasing agent ended the conversation by telling the program manager that she could find revised procedures in her company manual.

The purchasing department was eventually placed under the control of the operations department to provide for more timely response to suppliers.

In this example, the team's performance eventually suffered because (1) the team failed to see through the eyes of its customers, and (2) the team's systems, procedures, and work routines were set up for its own convenience, not those of its customers.

When you cut yourself off from your customers, you turn your greatest potential allies into your enemies. During tough times this is a dangerous and foolish thing to do. Customers have long memories. When they are called upon to evaluate your performance, their first response will be to review your record in supporting their requirements. This is particularly true of external customers, who, although further removed from your day-to-day operations, have even more impact on your professional life. The reputation that you establish with them will follow you throughout your career, long after you have left your current company.

During tough times you can't afford to become so preoccupied that you fail to gain perspective on your end results, nor can you ignore performance feedback from your internal customers. If you fall victim to either of these management roadblocks, you will quickly lose sight of your mission and purpose.

The most effective method for guarding against performance myopia is to obtain a second set of eyes and to use customer feedback to hone your team's performance. In this chapter you will be introduced to strategies, tactics, and tools to help you channel your team's time and effort into the critical performance areas and determine how well your team's performance meets the needs of your customers. Finally, you will be shown how to select the most effective method for initiating improvements and quickly identify those improvement options that are within the direct control of your team. By doing so, you will find it easier to balance your workload, shift through priorities, and more effectively focus your team's time and energy.

Warning Symptoms

The following warning symptoms can help you determine whether you are having difficulty focusing your team's efforts. Check those symptoms that apply to you.

- ❑ *Overwhelming work demands.* You feel overwhelmed by the amount of paper in your in-basket and the number of jobs facing you each day. Your team continually complains that it simply doesn't have the time needed to perform its work.
- ❑ *Conflicting priorities.* You find it hard to assess the relative importance of competing priorities and have difficulty determining the importance that your organization has attached to each of your responsibilities.
- ❑ *Conflicts with senior managers.* You just can't seem to convince your managers of the need to focus on jobs or projects that you know are critical to your team's survival.
- ❑ *Customer complaints.* You have been receiving an increasing number of complaints from your customers regarding the service your team provides.
- ❑ *Customers as competitors.* Your customers have begun to circumvent your group to get their needs met through other avenues. You've noticed the recent emergence of product or service gaps—areas in which customers' needs or requirements aren't being met by your team.

Strategies

When you are encountering tough times, you can't afford to spread your time and energy among competing priorities and projects. The first strategy we suggest, "Mapping" your customers, means stepping back from your daily activities to refocus your attention on those aspects of your work that are most important to your internal and external customers. It also means being able to anticipate how your team will need to evolve over time to meet changes in your customers' requirements.

Once you've identified your most critical performance areas, the second strategy, which we call "Driving a Chisel," involves determining how to initiate improvements effectively in these areas. A chisel is useful because it enables you to concentrate your effort over a narrow field, often the most vulnerable spot on a surface. Driving a chisel means clearly identifying those performance options that can be quickly implemented and that lie directly within your team's control and then using this information to determine how to focus your improvement efforts to obtain the best results.

Strategy 1: Map Your Customers

• **Focus on outputs, not activities.** To overcome the activity trap, you need first to distinguish clearly among your activities, outputs, and results. Activities are those tasks and functions that your team performs each day. For a financial analyst, they might be inputting budget data or checking budget variances against actuals; for a retail sales person, they might involve conducting inventories of merchandise or assisting customers with purchases.

Outputs are those products and services generated by your activities that serve the needs of your external and internal customers. Outputs may be information, documentation, parts, materials, service calls, or installations.

Results are the "value added" that your customers obtain from your outputs. For example, you can measure results in terms of the time service calls remain open, the time required to respond to phone inquiries, defect levels on parts, and the accuracy of budget forecasts. Customers aren't always impressed by your activities, and they may have little knowledge of how your team performs its activities. The only thing directly visible to your customers is your outputs, and customers' primary concern is the value they derive from your performance.

Ideally, activities should be selected on the basis of whether they support your most important outputs. However, people have a tendency to disregard importance and to focus instead on activities that they have traditionally performed. They also gravitate toward those activities that are the most comfortable and from which they derive the greatest enjoyment. Finally, people seldom take the time to systematically determine whether the team's efforts are focused on key outputs.

The activity trap reveals a lot about why managers are sometimes not fully appreciated or recognized in their organizations. How many times have you heard people say:

- I work harder and harder, but no one seems to care.
- If you want to see how much effort we're investing, just look at the data we've gathered.
- Our training group was very productive last year. We provided more than ten thousand hours of training.

These statements say nothing about results. They speak only of activities performed—which may or may not be related to key outputs. When you fall into the activity trap, you take great pride in the fact that you are working harder, regardless of whether you are actually getting anything accomplished through your efforts. As long as you put in extra hours, take on more work, and arrive home exhausted each day, you can convince yourself you are doing everything possible to improve your performance.

To find out whether you have fallen into the activity trap, ask yourself the following questions. Do you:

- Brag to friends and coworkers about how hard you work?
- Evaluate others' work performance by how much they sweat?
- Measure yourself against how much time you invest on activities (the more, the better)?
- Feel that you are not productive unless you feel stressed and fatigued?

If you've answered yes to these questions, you are probably focusing your efforts on activities rather than on the results you are able to obtain through them. On the other hand, do you:

- Measure yourself only against your end results?
- Continually look for ways to obtain good results while decreasing the time you spend on your activities?
- Look for ways to work smarter, not harder?
- Realize that putting in additional work hours does not automatically result in greater productivity?

If so, you are focusing your efforts on end results.

- **Measure what's important to your customers.** The second management trap is performance myopia—the failure to understand how your performance is viewed by your internal and external customers. To better understand how the activity trap and performance myopia interact to weaken your effectiveness, consider the recruiting section of a typical human resources department. Recruiters begin by obtaining necessary inputs from their customers (line managers), such as information on the numbers and types of positions to be filled and the desired qualifications of job candidates. From these inputs they perform a number of activities, including:

- Completing job requisition forms
- Screening job applications and resumés
- Interviewing applicants
- Recommending candidates to line managers
- Notifying candidates and internal departments of selection decisions

If the recruiting team has fallen into the activity trap, it will probably evaluate its performance in terms of the following activities:

- The number of applications processed
- The number of applicants interviewed
- The hours recruiters spent interviewing applicants

On the other hand, if the team is focused on results, it will measure its performance in terms of how well it is meeting its customers' requirements through its primary output—the delivery of qualified new hires to fill job openings. In this case, the department will be more likely to measure:

- Whether there is a good match between candidates' skills and job requirements. This is measured by the ratings that new hires receive on their six-month performance appraisals and the percentage of new hires who remain with the company for a full year.
- The cycle time required to bring new hires on board, measured either from the date job requisition forms are received to actual hiring dates or by the length of time that positions remain vacant.
- The cost of recruiting and hiring, measured by dividing the total cost of operating the recruiting department by the number of positions filled during the year.

The bottom line is that if the recruiting department wants to gain a reputation for being a high-performance group, it needs to measure its performance on key outputs, not activities. Regardless of how many job applications it screens or the number of people it interviews, the group won't be considered successful unless it can quickly obtain qualified job candidates. As a matter of fact, any extra time and effort spent on these activities will only be viewed as an additional nonvalue-added cost if the recruiters aren't getting the expected results.

A critical tool for measuring what's important to your customers is the Performance Map, explained in detail in the Tool Kit in this challenge. The Performance Map provides a detailed comparison of how you, your team, and your customers view the importance of your outputs and your team's performance of these outputs. In addition, the map can provide valuable clues about the best way to leverage performance—whether to increase, decrease, correct, or improve your team's efforts within each output.

• **Conduct customer interviews.** A simple but effective method for obtaining customer feedback is by the use of structured interviews. Your goal should be to come away with an informal "contract" between your team and customers that includes ways that you, your team, and your customers can work together better to strengthen performance and an agreed-upon method for periodically conducting joint reviews of your team's performance. The Customer Interview Guidelines in the Tool Kit should prove helpful in this area.

Strategy 2: Drive a Chisel

• **Start with quick kills.** Once your team has identified the most important areas for improvement, it will face the challenge of determining how to generate those improvements. The problem at this point is twofold. First, your team probably lacks the time, energy, and resources to implement more than a few improvement options. Second, you must convince your team to add still another responsibility (the improvement area) to its workload.

One way to overcome these problems is to use the Improvement Options Map in the Tool Kit in this chapter to brainstorm performance improvement options with your team and to determine the most effective approach for implementing each option. Each implementation approach should be based on the degree of control your team directly exerts over the improvement option and the relative speed of implementation for each option. Control is a function of several factors. Ask yourself:

- Does your team currently have the skills and experience needed to implement the improvement?
- Is the improvement option limited enough to be implemented with your staff and resources?
- Does your team have the authority to implement the improvement option?

Similarly, the speed at which an improvement option can be implemented depends on:

- The degree of coordination required among various groups to implement the improvement option.
- Whether the option can be undertaken only at certain stages of the company's fiscal year. For example, is it necessary to wait until the company's next annual review of new capital requests?
- The amount of work required to implement the improvement option.
- Whether the improvement option requires involvement and approval by a large number of stakeholders (employees, managers, customers, and support groups directly affected by or asked to support the implementation of the improvement option).
- The degree to which the desired improvement change will have a ripple effect on the performance of other areas downstream in the process. For example, engineering changes are sometimes made in products without first considering how these changes will affect how easy the product is to manufacture.

The purpose of this tactic is to size up quickly all potential improvement options and to flag those "quick kill" projects that can be most easily implemented by your team. By achieving rapid success in these areas, you can help your team gain motivation and momentum for more difficult improvement projects and also present your manager and customers with a clear signal about your commitment to improving your team's performance.

- **Select improvement options that provide payoffs for your team.** Once your improvement options are mapped, your team will have a better idea of which options can be easily implemented and which will require protracted effort. At this point, you may still have a number of potential improvement options on your plate. If you want to encourage team members to become excited about an improvement project, ask them to identify improvement options that, if implemented, would make their life easier. Would making an improvement help your team:
  - Eliminate unsafe work conditions?
  - Reduce tedious tasks?
  - Prevent frustrating rework?
  - Make a job less physically demanding?
  - Streamline cumbersome and time-consuming procedures?

Whenever possible, start with improvement projects that offer a win-win situation—improving both organizational performance and your team's work conditions.

• **Match efforts to payoffs.** Eliminate activities that don't directly add value to your customers and that are not essential to your operation. In providing consulting services to many *Fortune* 500 companies, I've found that often as much as 40 percent of a group's activities are only marginally related to its key processes. Unfortunately, a team's activities tend to grow exponentially over time, as the team assumes additional functions, damaged processes receive patches and mends rather than fundamental corrections, and procedures are made unnecessarily complicated. Like old clothes that have been stuffed in the back of a closet and ignored for years, many of these activities have been inherited from times gone by and are no longer needed.

The challenge here is to clean your closet. Take out for inventory each activity performed by your team; then eliminate those that are unnecessary and simplify the rest. To begin this process, I recommend starting with the Bull's-eye Exercise (discussed in detail in the Tool Kit in Challenge 5). This exercise can help you determine the relative importance of each of your team's activities. Whenever possible, marginal and unrelated activities should be eliminated. If elimination is impossible, your team needs to look for options for reducing the time it invests in these activities. Detailed guidelines for managing these types of nonvalue-added activities can be found in my book *Lifeboat Strategies: How to Keep Your Career Above Water During Tough Times—or Any Time* (New York: AMACOM, 1994).

TOOL KIT

Performance Map

I'm sure that you are familiar with the Pareto principle. This concept suggests that in many systems the majority of effects come from a relatively small number of causes. Management theorists refer to this as the 80/20 rule, meaning that often 80 percent of effects are attributable to only 20 percent of causes. For example, a sales organization may find that 20 percent of accounts provide at least 80 percent of total revenue. Or a manufacturing company may observe that 80 percent of defects are traceable to problems located in less than 20 percent of key processes.

The Pareto principle relies on separating the critical few causal factors from the trivial many. The Performance Map is one tool you can use to identify those critical few outputs that are most important

to your internal and external customers. It is an excellent tool for identifying effective ways to focus your team's efforts.

The map consists of ratings provided by you, your team, and your
customers on a two-dimensional grid. (Later in this challenge we discuss applying it to your managers and suppliers.) The vertical axis is
used to rate the relative importance of each output by assigning a rating from 1 to 7, with 7 being extremely important and 1 being least
important.

The horizontal axis allows you and your customers to compare
how you view your team's performance on different outputs, using
the same 1–7 scale. A rating of 7 means that performance is excellent
in a given area; a rating of 1 means that performance is unacceptable.

The use of the importance and performance rating scales enable
you to place each output into one of four quadrants, as shown in Figure 3-1.

- *Increase* (upper right quadrant). These are outputs that are extremely important and on which you are performing well. You
  should attempt to increase your current efforts on these outputs.

Figure 3-1. The Performance Map.

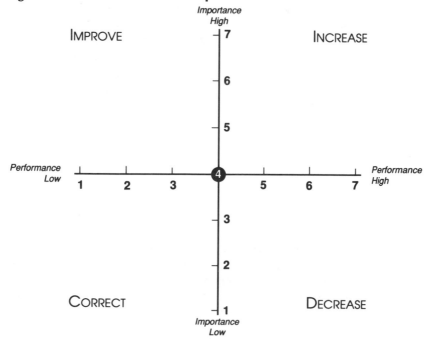

- *Decrease* (lower right quadrant). These are outputs that are not very important but on which you are performing well. You should decrease your current work efforts on these outputs. These are the things that you are doing for your customers, regardless of whether they want them ("Eat it, it's good for you!").
- *Improve* (upper left quadrant). These are outputs that are very important and on which you are not performing well. You should strive to make major improvements to these outputs. Outputs that fall into this quadrant pose the greatest performance improvement challenges to your team.
- *Correct* (lower left quadrant). These are outputs that are not very important and on which you are not performing well. You should attempt to make minor corrections to these outputs but should not expend a great deal of time and effort on them.

Interpreting Results

The Performance Map provides you with a useful reality test for evaluating your performance. By comparing the gap between how you and your customers view your work on a particular output, you can learn where to redirect your efforts for better results. Let's review some examples.

In the first example (Figure 3-2), let's consider that your team has rated a particular output 7 on importance and 6 on performance, although your customer has rated this same output 7 on importance but 2 on performance. Obviously, you both agree that the output is very important; however, your team's performance in this area falls quite short of your customers' expectation.

Now what if these ratings were reversed—if you both agreed on the importance but you rated the output performance as 2 although your customers rated it as 7? This profile could suggest that you are more dissatisfied with your performance than are your customers. Is this a problem? Perhaps.

This profile sometimes occurs when part of your performance is hidden from your customer. For example, the president of a major manufacturing company once told me that although his customer was very pleased about the quality of his company's products, the customer did not know that the company was experiencing very significant quality problems. To hide this problem from the customer, the company was performing 100 percent inspection of all its products (thousands per month) immediately before they went out the door to

Figure 3-2. Example 1 of the Performance Map.

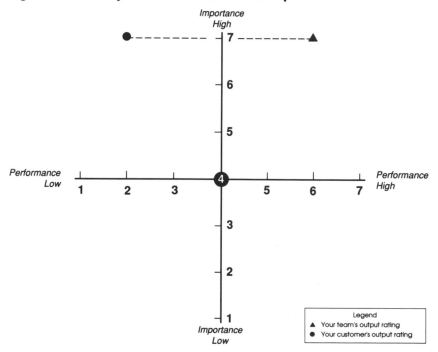

the customer. In reality, almost 20 percent of all products were failing the inspection process.

A second way of interpreting these score differences is that you may be a perfectionist who continues to see room for improvement, even when your customer is perfectly satisfied. Is this a problem? Only if your constant "improvements" involve a high level of cost and excessive time delays without generating improvements that are appreciated by your customers.

Finally, this gap may be occurring because you are in a position to anticipate needed changes to your products and services. For example, if you are responsible for materials management you may be planning to overhaul your procedures for transporting hazardous chemicals, even though your internal customer (the production department) is perfectly happy with your procedures. Why? Because you know that impending changes in federal regulations will place increased restrictions on the transport of such chemicals, and you believe that your procedures will need to be modified accordingly. In this case, your challenge will be to provide customer education to explain to

your customer the advantages of raising its performance standards for
your outputs.

Now let's review another example (Figure 3-3). On this map you
have rated a key output as 4 in importance and 6 in performance, and
your customers have rated that same output 6 in importance and 5 in
performance.

In this case, the gap may be occurring because you don't understand how important your output is to your customers. For example,
some members of a team were upset that their two new file clerks were
creating bottlenecks in processing certain documentation. During a
team-building exercise, it became apparent that the file clerks were
never really informed that processing these documents was a mandatory step in finalizing new customer accounts and that any delay held
up other departments. Once they knew the importance of timely processing to their internal customers, they responded with new ideas for
speeding up their output.

On the other hand, let's consider a situation in which you both
generally agreed on the output's performance but you gave the output
6 and your customers gave it 4 in importance. This might mean that

Figure 3-3. Example 2 of the Performance Map.

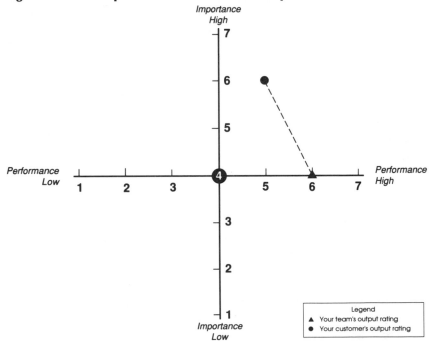

your customers disregard the importance that you place on your outputs.

This situation often occurs when your customers don't understand the full value of your outputs. For example, a colleague told me that some of her company's first-line managers were not very supportive of a new performance appraisal training program. Those opinions changed once the training department took the time to explain that the training was important because the company would soon be giving first-line managers greater say in recommending performance ratings. Again, in this situation the key is to educate your customers regarding the importance of your outputs.

Applying the Performance Map

In this section, we look at how a hypothetical team might use the mapping process from beginning to end, from the big picture to details, with multiple customers, multiple outputs, and a competitor.

A customer service team requested importance and performance ratings from three key external customers on the following five service outputs:

1. *Output A.* On-site service support
2. *Output B.* Technical training programs for customers
3. *Output C.* Response to information requests
4. *Output D.* Response to service calls
5. *Output E.* Response to complaints

In addition, the team asked its customers to rate a primary competitor's performance in the same five service areas. Once it received the ratings, the team created a feedback form and averaged the numbers to obtain an overall score profile (Figure 3-4). Finally, they plotted the team's and the competitor's performance rating on a Performance Map using different symbols (Figure 3-5).

From this map, the team could form the following conclusions:

• The team discovered the degree to which its three key customers agreed on the importance of each output. The team decided to focus its efforts on outputs that were rated as important to all customers, such as the team's ability to respond to service calls (D) and on-site service support (A). Activities that are viewed as being exceptionally important by all your customers receive an inordinate amount of visi-

Figure 3-4. The Feedback Form.

Symbol	Service Area (Output)	Importance Ratings				Performance Ratings				
		Customers			Avg.	Customers			Avg.	Competitors
		X	Y	Z		X	Y	Z		
A	On-site service support	6	7	6	6.33	7	6	7	6.66	3
B	Technical training	4	5	4	4.33	6	5	5	5.33	5
C	Response to info requests	3	6	3	4.00	5	5	6	5.33	3
D	Response to service calls	6	7	7	6.66	3	2	2	2.33	6
E	Response to complaints	5	5	5	5.00	7	6	5	6.00	5.5

Figure 3-5. Example 3 of the Performance Map.

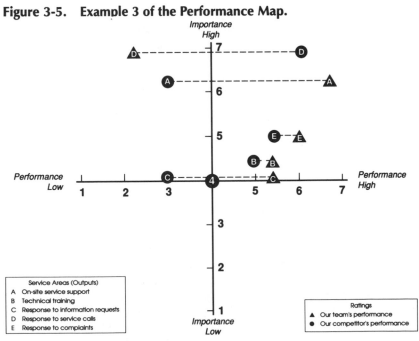

Service Areas (Outputs)
A On-site service support
B Technical training
C Response to information requests
D Response to service calls
E Response to complaints

Ratings
▲ Our team's performance
● Our competitor's performance

bility. For better or worse, these are the activities that cast you into the spotlight in your organization.

- The team was able to identify areas in which its customers expressed widely different needs. For example, the team might find it useful to determine why Customer Y viewed information requests (C) as very important, even though Customers X and Z viewed that factor as only moderately important. Customer Y may have placed greater emphasis on this output because it lacks a solid understanding of how to install and operate the suppliers' products and is more dependent on effective follow-up support. On the other hand, Customer Y's high rating on this area may indicate that this customer receives less initial information from the product installation team assigned to this region and therefore requires more handholding after product installations.

- The map also shows how customers view the team's performance on each service area. For example, it indicated that in the most important service area, the team's ability to respond effectively to service calls, the team's performance was rated poor.

- Finally, the team was able to identify areas in which it was leading and in which it was falling behind its chief competitor. For example, the team realized that it was lagging in the area of responding to service calls (D) but was doing better in providing on-site service support (A).

Analyzing Customers' Requirements

Now that the team has the overall performance picture, let's see how it can take a closer look. The Performance Map can be used to help you identify specific improvement opportunities—areas where your customers' expectations or requirements are not met. Measures of customer expectations might include:

- *Accuracy/defects*—the degree to which defects or errors are present in your work
- *Timeliness*—how long it takes for you to complete work or provide service
- *Completeness*—the degree to which your work contains all required parts, materials, or information
- *Reliability*—the degree to which you can be counted on to perform as expected
- *Serviceability*—whether your product is easy to repair or self-service

- *Cost*—both initial cost and any on-going expenses required to maintain your product or service

In order to obtain an accurate understanding of your customer's requirements, it's important for you to encourage your customers to describe their requirements in specific, unambiguous, and measurable terms. When this accuracy is missing, problems occur. Here is a real-life example.

What is meant by the term *delivery date?* A manufacturer ran into problems because it defined on-schedule shipments as those that left the shipping docks on time. Its customers, however, tracked shipment arrival times. Delays caused by ineffective shipping and handling were therefore hidden from the manufacturer's view. Implicit in this measurement was the manufacturer's idea that "if we get it out the door on time, we've completed our responsibility."

In this example, job performance improved and relationships with customers were strengthened when managers reached agreement with their customers on how requirements should be defined and measured.

Now let's continue with our example of the customer service team. One of the team's most important outputs was its response to service calls. Again, the team requested performance and importance ratings from its three key customers on four requirements for this output:

1. *Requirement 1.* Timeliness of initial response. How much time elapsed from the moment service calls were received to the arrival of service representatives at the site. (Customers' Rating Average: Importance 6.5; Performance 5)
2. *Requirement 2.* Service time. The time service calls remained open; the time required to complete repairs once service representatives were at the site. (Customers' Rating Average: Importance 7; Performance 2)
3. *Requirement 3.* Friendliness and courtesy. Whether the service representative smiled, responded to questions, avoided tracking dirt into the customer's office, etc. (Customers' Rating Average: Importance 6; Performance 6.5)
4. *Requirement 4.* Reliability. Whether the service was performed properly the first time without the need for repeated call-backs. (Customers' Rating Average: Importance 6.5; Performance 6)

The team then plotted this data onto a new Performance Map (Figure 3-6). From these customer ratings, the team learned that the most important thing that it could do was to improve its service time. Customers were upset that service often took longer than anticipated and frequently carried over from one day to the next.

In summary, the Performance Map can provide a variety of useful information:

- If you lack the staff, resources, or time needed to accomplish all your work, the map can help you identify your work priorities.
- It encourages your customers to provide clear and specific performance feedback by helping suppliers and customers pinpoint areas of initial disagreement regarding whether work is being performed according to agreed-upon requirements.
- It enables you to benchmark your performance against the performance of your competitors or best-in-field performers.
- It can help you monitor your performance.
- It can be used to demonstrate to your managers and customers

Figure 3-6. Example 4 of the Performance Map.

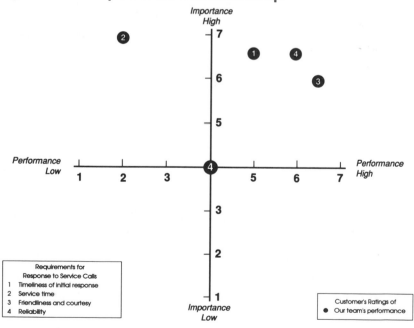

Requirements for
Response to Service Calls
1 Timeliness of initial response
2 Service time
3 Friendliness and courtesy
4 Reliability

Customer's Ratings of
● Our team's performance

areas in which you have made strong performance improvements.

Applying the Performance Map to Your Team

As your team begins to look for ways to increase its effectiveness, keep in mind some general guidelines. If your customers and manager don't agree with how you view the importance of your outputs and requirements, the reason may be that:

- You have knowledge they don't yet possess regarding the potential impact of good or poor performance in this work area
- You are closer to the problem or more technically proficient (a problem of educating the customer)
- You don't understand your customers' requirements
- Your customers' requirements and priorities may be changing rapidly
- You may be focusing on short-term requirements, while your customer is considering the long-term impact of this work area, or vice versa

If your customers don't agree with you on how you view your performance on outputs and requirements, it may be that:

- You don't understand their requirements
- You may not have timely, accurate feedback on your performance in these areas (conversely, they may not have access to performance feedback obtained by your team)
- Their performance standards may be changing
- They may be benchmarking your team's current performance against the performance of other, best-in-field competitors, whereas you are measuring your team's current performance against its past performance

Customer Interview Guidelines

The following guidelines are useful when interviewing your customer to identify ways to improve your team's performance.

Prior to Meeting with Your Customer

1. Put together a simple outline of the steps that your team goes through to provide specific products or services for your customer.

2. Complete the Performance Map with your team, and invite members to suggest issues they would like to see addressed during the discussion.
3. Have your customer complete a map for one or all of your most important outputs.
4. Note any examples of situations in which communication breakdowns have occurred between you and your customer over lack of definition on outputs or requirements.

During the Meeting

1. Don't position the discussion as a finger-pointing session. It is not productive to have each side focus on past problems. Explain to your customer that you are searching for ways to strengthen your team's performance by becoming more responsive and by looking for ways to build better communication between your respective teams.
2. Start by inviting your customer to share his or her responses to these questions:

• *How are we doing?* This open-ended question is a good starting point for discussion. It encourages customers to open up and freely discuss your performance, and it tells them that you are interested in hearing their views.

• *What do you like about what we are doing? What should we not change?* This question ensures that you don't make the mistake of "throwing the baby out with the bath water" when you begin to plan ways to improve your work. Your customers' answers also can help you justify to your managers why you are investing resources on certain projects and efforts at the expense of others.

• *Are any of our procedures or documentation difficult to understand or apply?* In other words, are our work procedures user-friendly? Can they be easily understood by everyone in the department? Sometimes customers are reluctant to explain that they don't understand how to interpret company or departmental procedures or technical specialties.

• *What changes could we make in the way we provide products or services that would make life easier for you?* You may be unintentionally creating additional work problems for your customers by the way you deliver services to them. An engineer friend of mine was very surprised when it was pointed out to him that because he had gotten into the bad habit of sloppily sketching his requirements for part designs, the production department was forced to waste time and rework trying to interpret his notes.

• *Is there any additional support you need from us?* Your customers may assume you aren't providing services because you don't have the skills or resources to do so. As a result, they may attempt to get them from the outside—a move that may place you in direct competition with your customers.

• *Have you noticed any changes in our service lately?* As a manager you should consider this key question. Your customer can alert you to the emergence of service problems and to areas in which your team has made important improvements in service delivery.

• *Are your needs and requirements likely to change over the next year? How can our team help you meet these changes?* Requirements are always a moving target. For example, perhaps you currently mail documentation to another division in your company. If this internal customer is under pressure to find ways to respond faster to its own customers, it may soon require you to expedite shipments or information through overnight express, fax, or modem. Or it may feel that even though it will continue to need your services, upcoming budget reductions will soon make these services unaffordable unless you can help it find ways to contain costs. In short, if you want to keep your customers satisfied, you have to plan now for projected changes in their requirements.

• *What is one thing we can do to improve our relationship with you?* This question often provides information on soft criteria—critical customer requirements that may not surface unless you specifically probe for them. For example, several women colleagues of mine have told me that on many occasions they have been irritated by the patronizing treatment they have received from salesmen in car dealerships. This frustration is not something that is likely to surface in dealers' customer surveys, but it will certainly influence dealers' success.

• *Is there anything that you could tell us about your operation that would make it easier for us to support your efforts? Is there anything that you feel you need to know about how we perform our work?* Often internal departments run into conflicts because they simply don't understand how their efforts affect those of other departments. One of the fastest ways to improve your work is for you and your customers to become more knowledgeable about how each of you performs your work.

3. If you find that the discussion is becoming sidetracked over personal issues, try to translate these issues into performance problems. For example:

    Customer: And another thing that you've got to do is take control of Pete. My people feel that he's rude and arrogant.

    Supplier: Can you tell me a little more about how he comes across when he acts like that? It would help me coach him on this area.

    Customer: Well, whenever any of us ask if something can be done, he cuts us off and immediately says something like "There's no way we can do that" without even hearing us out. He never listens to our ideas or bothers to explain why he can't do things a certain way. He acts as if he's above it all.

    Supplier: So one thing that you'd like to be able to expect from any of my team is that they come across as friendly and responsive, specifically, that they listen completely to your requests and that they explain their rationale for why they might not be able to meet all of your requests. Is that it?

    Customer: Exactly.

4. Explain to your customers any steps that they could take to make it easier for you to meet their requirements. For example, I directed a team building workshop for two departments—the supplier had the responsibility of providing the customer with a monthly evaluation of the feasibility of purchasing certain parcels of real estate. The customer started the discussion by complaining that the written analysis was seldom received on time from the supplier. The supplier explained that it would make a firm commitment to meet the monthly deadline but that in order to do so it needed the customer's help. Up to that point, the customer had generated three different types of data, which had been presented on a piecemeal basis to the supplier from three different groups within the customer's department. The supplier explained that it could speed up its delivery time if these data were first consolidated by the customer and presented to the supplier in a single format. At the end of the team building session, each team left with a series of actions it could take to support its partner.

Improvement Options Map

We have discussed how you can use the Performance Map (Figure 3-1) to obtain accurate customer feedback on your performance. We have also explained that you can best leverage your performance by trying to make improvements in those outputs that fall into the Increase quadrant of the map. Once you've accomplished this, you can use the map to identify for each Increase output those requirements that need the greatest improvement. The question you now face is how to make improvements to these key requirements most effectively.

The Improvement Options Map (Figure 3-7) can help you answer this question. This mapping process is the same one we used with the Performance Map, plotting the 1–7 ratings on a two-dimensional grid. The only difference is that the ratings are made in new categories.

The vertical axis records the degree of control your team has in implementing a requirement improvement. Improvement options that receive high scores (6–7) are considered to be entirely within your team's control. Options receiving moderate scores (3–5) can be influenced only indirectly by your team, and those with low scores (1–2) are almost completely outside your team's control.

Figure 3-7. The Improvement Options Map.

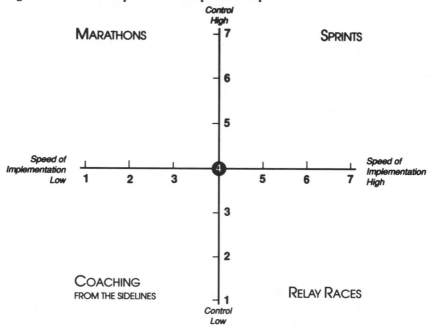

The horizontal axis of the map reflects the speed of implementation for improvement options. High-scoring (6–7) options can be implemented quickly, whereas those with moderate scores (3–5) take longer to implement and those with low scores (1–2) require a long time for implementation.

Once again, when the requirement's improvement options have been rated, the numbers get plotted into four quadrants.

1. *Sprints* (upper right quadrant). These are improvement options that can be easily controlled and implemented by your team. I recommend that any improvement project begin with the implementation of these options. By achieving rapid success in these areas, you help your team gain momentum for more difficult improvement projects and also present your manager and customers with a clear signal that you are committed to improving your team's performance. In addition, it doesn't hurt to see how far your team can go on improving its performance before investing additional time and effort on other improvement options.

2. *Marathons* (upper left quadrant). These options are also within your team's control but require extended effort over a longer period of time for implementation. Watch any marathon and you can easily spot the first-time runners. These are the people who eagerly sprint across the first few miles of the race. Not having learned to pace themselves over the long run, they quickly become tired and discouraged. The secret of successfully implementing marathon projects is to have a detailed game plan for making improvements. (Such projects also require a higher investment of time and energy from your team.) You may find the Project Planning Worksheet (the last tool in this kit) helpful in attacking marathon improvement projects.

3. *Relay Races* (lower right quadrant). These are improvement projects that can be easily implemented but that are largely outside the control of your team. They require the support, assistance, or approval of other managers or teams. The most important elements in winning a relay race are timing and delegation. Translated for the improvement process, this means being able to determine the best time and approach for handing off improvement projects to other groups. Again, the Project Planning Worksheet may be useful in helping you select the best approach for dealing with your key stakeholders—those who will be affected the most by the improvements you would like to make.

4. *Sideline Coaching* (lower left quadrant). These are the most difficult improvement projects. They take a long time to complete and can

be undertaken only by key managers or groups outside your team. For example, you may need to ask your internal suppliers to help your team's performance by making changes in their work processes.

As with Relay Races, a key ingredient in the success of any Sideline Coaching project is your ability to win over the support of your stakeholders. In addition, because these projects require a much longer completion time, you also need to consider methods for tracking progress and, sometimes, for prodding key stakeholders toward project completion.

When improvements are poorly implemented, it's often because the managers who have undertaken those improvements have misinterpreted where improvement options fall on the map. The following example, provided by Ed Nolan, training director for Eckerd Drug Company, shows what happens when a improvement project that requires Sideline Coaching is treated as a Marathon project without considering project stakeholders.[1]

> Last August we had a major reorganization of the company. Some of our long-term plans involved developing software support systems for our VPs, which would replace some of our required clerical staff. The person who was responsible for eliminating the clericals picked a date of nine months out, when he felt it would occur. He let this deadline drive his behavior, and when some changes occurred in the project to prolong it, he didn't adjust the deadline.
>
> The interesting thing was that this person was developing this project with a lot of partners, including data processing, training, sales and cash, and accounting. He had all of these people together but refused to accept their input. As it turned out, with all of the information he was given, he was repeatedly told that the deadline couldn't be met, but he kept saying, "No, I have a deadline to meet. It will work." This became a bad project that no one could put the brakes on. He missed the deadline radically, and it caused tremendous disruption in the field, because he was driven by the deadline and not the realities of the situation.

You can use the Improvement Options Map to:

1. Map out improvement options with your team, and select initial options for consideration.

2. Obtain feedback regarding how key stakeholders view the improvement options identified by your team.
3. Benchmark other managers by having them plot on the map where they would place similar performance improvement projects they have successfully completed. This will provide you with information regarding the relative degree of difficulty you can expect to encounter if you replicate any of these improvement projects.
4. Facilitate team building with other groups. When working on a joint improvement project, your separate teams can individually plot on the map where they would place different improvement options. Frequently, this approach can help you reach consensus regarding where to begin improvement efforts and how to red-flag improvement options that are viewed quite differently by your respective teams.

Project Planning Worksheet

The Project Planning Worksheet (Figure 3-8) is an excellent tool for troubleshooting project activities. Follow these steps when completing the worksheet:

1. *Project Summary.* At the top of the worksheet provide a brief summary of the improvement project.

2. *Project Steps.* In the spaces from left to right, list the major steps that you think will be required to complete the project.

3. *Estimated Time Frame.* Describe both the specific start and stop dates for each project step and the amount of time that you think will be required to complete each step.

4. *Resources Needed.* Describe the resources that will be required to complete each step of the project. A sample list is given on the worksheet. Give special attention to resources such as facilities, which require advanced scheduling or coordination.

5. *Stakeholders.* Identify and list those persons and/or groups who will be significantly affected by the improvement project or the completion of a given stage of the project. This might include senior managers, managers of other functions, customers, suppliers, or staff support. You now need to determine how these people will need to be involved. Do they simply need to be informed after the fact that a

Figure 3-8. The Project Planning Worksheet.

Project summary:			page __ of __
Project steps →	①	②	③
Estimated time frame			
Resources needed • Time • Equipment/facilities • Parts / materials • Computers / software • Training			
Stakeholders • Who will be affected? • What technical help do we need? • Whose approval is required to proceed?			
Problems anticipated • Resistance • Lack of data • Coordination • Technical • Time Investment			

change is in progress, or should you work on getting their buy-in prior to implementing the change? Do you need firm commitments from them for help or support before you can begin a certain stage of the project? Can they serve as technical experts or troubleshooters for a certain step? Is their approval required for a certain stage of project completion?

6. *Problems Anticipated.* List problems that you think you may encounter in completing each stage of the project. These problems may include resistance from other managers or groups, the need to proceed with inadequate data, problems in coordination, the need for specialized technical assistance, or the need for a concentrated investment of time by your team.

Obtaining the buy-in and support of your stakeholders is probably one of the most important parts of a well-developed plan. Terry Geraghty, director of organizational development for Harris Electronic Systems Sector, offers this advice:

At my sector in Harris we are going from a centralized mind-set to a decentralized function. What this means for someone in a staff position like me is that things are different. In the old days, when our managers said, "We are going left," my job was to determine how to get us there the fastest. Nowadays, when the decision is to go left, my job is to go out and build consensus and educate, persuade, and convince people that it's to their best interest to go left. And the personal learning for me is that the time spent selling a plan is more important than the purity of the design.[2]

The Project Planning Worksheet has many valuable applications:

- Consider having different members complete the worksheet and then consolidating this information on a single form. This can help ensure good communication among members and serves as a troubleshooting activity.
- Use the worksheet as a planning guide for less experienced members and to facilitate project reviews with these members.
- Post the worksheet, and assign a team member to update it weekly for better communications.
- Select other managers as troubleshooters for your project. Review your completed worksheet with them, and ask them to help you probe for potential holes in your project plan.
- Under Problems Anticipated, you may find it useful to rate each of your problem entries on a scale of 1 to 5 so that you can red-flag critical problem areas for later review.
- If you are engaging in a benchmarking study, provide the benchmarked group with a copy of your completed worksheet and ask for its suggestions for revising the sheet on the basis of the group's own success stories.
- Each time you complete a step of your improvement project, go back to your original worksheet and revise it on the basis of what you have learned. Create a "Lessons Learned" file that your team can later refer to when working on other, similar projects.
- You might find it useful to highlight all information on your worksheet that is based on unverified assumptions. For example, you might assume that your team will require some specified technical training to complete a certain step when, in fact, this technical support could be easily provided by other groups. Then create a list of steps you can take to test these assumptions.

Notes

1. Interview with Ed Nolan, training director for Eckerd Drug Company, May 1993.
2. Interview with Terry Geraghty, director of organizational development for Harris Electronic Systems Sector, March 1993.

Challenge 4

Inspire the Troops

Gaining Full Commitment from Your Team

So here you are, caught in a nutcracker. Your manager is screaming for your group to be more productive, and you know that your team's performance is being scrutinized. You recognize that to meet your organization's rising performance expectations you will need to gain the full commitment of each of your team members. You, of course, are not concerned about this, for, having read the preceding chapters, you are now armed with a series of powerful techniques for improving your team's performance. Obviously, your team will give you its full support, right?

In the process of gaining full commitment from your team you are likely to encounter three obstacles.

1. *Current changes in the marketplace, including the loss of job security and increasingly stringent performance standards, are forcing a radical shift in how professionals view their jobs.* These changes involve alterations in the psychological contract that has traditionally existed between employees and their organizations.

As Harold Burlingame, senior vice president of human resources for AT&T, explains it:

> There was a time when someone would come to the front door of AT&T and see an invisible sign that said, AT&T: A JOB FOR LIFE. That's over. Now it's a shared kind of thing. Come to us. We'll invest in you, and you invest in us. Together, we'll face the market, and the degree to which we succeed will determine how things work out.[1]

These changing expectations come as a big shock to individuals who have come to expect job security, frequent promotions, and automatic merit increases as rewards for past corporate loyalty. Their secret hope is that the new company push for greater productivity will be just another of the many organizational campaigns that have quickly come and gone. They believe that if they just sit tight and hold on, things will soon revert to normal. To gain full commitment from your team, you need to address these assumptions and establish performance expectations that accurately reflect the changing requirements of your organization.

2. *Team members feel that they are already pushing as hard as they can.* After all, aren't they doing more than they did last year? Haven't they occasionally skipped lunch and put in extra hours? What do you want, blood? To gain full effort from your team you will need to challenge the performance limits that your team has set for itself, and show members that they are capable of greater contributions.

3. *People are reluctant to move out of their comfort zones.* Imagine a melting iceberg. The center of the iceberg represents each employee's comfort zone—the area of responsibilities and projects with which employees are most comfortable and that use their strongest skills. In order to gain top performance from your team, you will have to convince members to move from the center of the iceberg to its outer edges by asking them to take over the responsibilities of other displaced workers, display greater initiative to identify performance improvement opportunities, and develop new technical skills.

Unfortunately, while it's true that people want to grow in their jobs, this drive is counterbalanced by the fear of failure people experience whenever they are pushed to new performance levels. This is especially true in today's tough business environment, where the perceived risk level for failure has risen sharply for many professionals. When companies undertake downsizings or reorganizations, employees fear that their icebergs are melting, and they dash for the security of their comfort zones. As Patrick Miller, director of human resources for TECO Transport and Trade, explains: "The average employee is becoming more informed and learning more about the company. As he does, he often discovers some harsh economic realities, which drives him from empowerment to the sub-basement of economic uncertainty."[2]

In confronting this obstacle, your challenge will be to encourage members to take the risk of moving toward greater self-direction and initiative.

These three obstacles—members' increased fear of failure, their belief that they've already reached the limits of their performance, and their reluctance to move out of their comfort zones—must be overcome if you want your team to give you its full effort and commitment. In this chapter we discuss how to capture this effort through the strategies of overcoming inertia and encouraging members to challenge their limits. In addition, we look at how, by applying these strategies, you can help members achieve a greater degree of personal control over their jobs and careers.

Warning Symptoms

The following warning symptoms may indicate that lack of commitment and effort is rapidly becoming a critical management issue for your team:

❑ Your members leave as soon as possible after quitting time each day and refuse to work overtime when needed.

❑ Members doubt their ability to perform. They feel overwhelmed by small challenges and routinely gripe about the lack of fairness in assignments.

❑ Members seem to feel that "it's every person for herself." They are unwilling to help each other on projects or to assist each other in problem solving.

❑ Whenever you ask members to take on new assignments or skill areas, their first reaction is to offer excuses why they can't be expected to handle these new job challenges.

❑ You feel that your team is performing well below its maximum performance potential.

Strategies

The first strategy is to overcome inertia. An engineering friend once explained that 90 percent of a locomotive's energy is expended during the first few minutes of start-up as it attempts to move the train from rest. Once the engine overcomes its massive inertia and the train is running at high speed, relatively small amounts of energy are needed to keep it in motion. In much the same way, the first job you must tackle will be to overcome your team's initial inertia and get it started along the track. In this section we offer strategies for overcoming inertia by creating a sense of urgency, removing yourself as a buffer, conducting a performance analysis, and creating competitors.

The second strategy is to challenge the limits of your members. In the introduction to this chapter I mentioned the obstacle of members who assume that they are working to the limits of their capability. This strategy involves encouraging your members to raise their self-expectations, redefining performance, modeling limit-busting, cloning superstars, and using incremental successes and celebrations.

The last strategy is to get out of the way of team members. This involves removing any roadblocks that you may be unintentionally placing in their path. Managers get in the way whenever they hamstring a team's authority and its control over its own work, send inconsistent messages about desired performance, or create consequences that actually work against desired performance. As part of getting out of the way, you will discover how to strategically empower your staff, send clear messages about your performance expectations, and create consequences that support desired performance.

Strategy 1: Overcome Inertia

Create a sense of urgency. The first tactic for helping your team overcome inertia is to convince members that their survival and success depend on their ability to act now to make dramatic improvements in their performance. The importance of creating a sense of urgency can't be overestimated. It's a key tactic applied by some of the world's best organizational change strategists.

In his excellent book *The Breakthrough Strategy: Using Short-Term Successes to Build the High-Performance Organization*, Robert Schaffer says, "Begin with an *urgent* and *compelling* goal. The focus should be on improvements that everybody will clearly and instantly recognize as vital and necessary *now*, and that are therefore capable of arousing some zest."[3] Similarly, in his book on organizational change, *Teaching the Elephant to Dance: The Manager's Guide to Empowering Change*, James Belasco offers this advice: "Build a sense of urgency. Bad situations motivate change. Very bad situations. Pain and anxiety create the urgency to change, which creates the empowerment for change. Don't create this urgency, and people feel powerless to change."[4] Finally, consider what Judith Bardwick has to say in her book, *Danger in the Comfort Zone: From Boardroom to Mailroom—How to Break the Entitlement Habit That's Killing American Business*, about the tactics required to push individuals out of the "psychology of entitlement":

The only way to energize lethargic organizations and people is to push them into the psychology of Earning. It usually takes some shaking up—perhaps even a crisis. But after years of avoiding risk, people find any risk frightening. It is important to remember that when there is a lot of entitlement, any movement toward Earning, even if it is small, feels like Fear at first. That's why we say that any movement out of deep Entitlement toward Earning also means moving first into Fear. And that's precisely why it's so hard. . . . Senior managers will need great courage and toughness. It takes courage to sustain the pressure long enough so people truly realize Entitlement is over.[5]

The difficult question is how to generate a sense of urgency within a team that has become complacent. I don't think that this can be done by passing along the latest executive memo on the state of the organization or by the use of thinly veiled threats and intimidation. Threats and grandiose statements about the need for greater productivity are not effective motivators. Instead, try the following tactics:

- Give team members the opportunity to discover for themselves how important it is to meet the organization's rapidly changing performance expectations. The Crystal Ball Exercise (discussed in the Tool Kit) provides an effective method for guiding this type of exploratory discussion.
- Make use of the close-call phenomenon. Perhaps you know of another group or division that has already experienced considerable difficulties (staff or budget reductions, loss of management positions) as the result of performance problems like those just beginning to plague your team. If so, put your team in touch with these groups to discuss their lessons learned. Afterward, pull your team together and discuss how to avoid these problems.
- Benchmark your team's performance against other teams inside your company or other organizations. Toyota executives recognized that to make the transition to luxury cars, they had to first show their employees the more demanding customer requirements of the luxury car market. To drive home this point, they transported busloads of employees to the Nagota golf course and encouraged them to examine closely the Mercedes, Porches, Jaguars, and BMWs in the parking lot. By encouraging the examination of everything from paint finishes to metal frames,

Toyota made a very eloquent statement about the performance jump that was needed to produce a car of comparable quality.[6]

Remove yourself as a buffer. If a team doesn't seem committed to change, it may be because members have been insulated from exposure to performance problems. If you find that you are being overly protective of your team, try the following tactics:

- Let your team hear directly from your customers about the need for performance improvement. This may require meetings with your customers, visits to customer sites to see firsthand the difficulties customers are having with your products or services, or having one of your customers complete a Performance Map (Challenge 3) for several of your team's outputs.
- Show your team the result of performance problems. The production manager of a manufacturing company accomplished this by taking engineering and production people through his shop's quarantine area (the area reserved for defective products) and then explaining the amount of money that was being lost through these defects.

Set up a performance monitoring project. Select an important performance area that is not currently being tracked (e.g., response time to customers, shipping schedules, quality of service calls). Ask members to give you a rough estimate of their performance in this area, then challenge them to track their performance for one month. Teams often significantly overestimate their actual performance. Watching a trend line veer away from an overly optimistic performance estimate can be a sobering experience.

Conduct a performance analysis. In this tactic the steps of a work process are outlined on a flowchart and the team then identifies performance steps that are prone to errors and bottlenecks or are overly complicated. One reason that performance analysis is a great motivator is that it opens up processes to review by and feedback from a broad cross section of your organization. As a team motivational tool, performance analysis is particularly useful when:

- Members are stuck at a performance plateau because of poorly designed or overly cumbersome processes.
- Members have difficulty identifying performance problems because they are too close to the process. They have stopped paying attention to the problems created by inefficiencies and have fallen into the habit of working around ineffective processes.
- Problems are partially hidden because they occur at cross-over points—points where work flows across the boundaries be-

tween your team and other groups. Each team assumes that the problem is the other's responsibility.

Take away your team's safety net. Safety nets are an added bit of protection that teams try to provide themselves by padding schedules or intentionally operating staff, equipment, and resources at levels below full utilization. Years ago, my safety net was removed. As a management trainer, I was one of three team members delivering a series of management programs. Within three months, my two coworkers were transferred, and I was told to maintain the same level of training. At first I thought that this would be impossible, but then I forced myself to review systematically everything I did and to identify those responsibilities that were critical to my survival. I shortened some classes, packed more people into others, eliminated all nonessential activities, and assigned some training courses to an outside consultant. As a result, I surpassed my previous year's training level and later received my company's productivity award.

Safety nets are a bit like bicycle training wheels; once you are able to keep yourself going without them your self-confidence rises and they are quickly discarded. In my case, once I saw the new level of performance I was able to attain, I began to raise my own expectations for my performance. What safety nets have you placed under your people? What would happen if you temporarily removed them? For example, could you juggle around assignments to maintain your current workload during vacation periods? Could you challenge your team to make do without resources on which it's traditionally relied? Set a goal to eliminate any safety nets that may be discouraging your staff from performing at its best.

Create a competitor for your team. In my experience, teams often suffer from complacency because they've been shielded from competition. Judith Bardwick offers the example of Square D corporation, an electrical equipment manufacturer, which has a scoreboard in its corporate headquarters that displays information on how the company is performing against its competitors, such as General Electric and Westinghouse.[7]

Use the following ideas to create a competitor for your team:

- Invite bids from outside vendors who offer services competitive with those provided by your team. Force your team to conduct a detailed make/buy analysis proving that it can match the quality, response time, and cost offered by these vendors. Performing a comparative cost analysis will help your team better understand the overhead costs it represents to your company.

- Sponsor competitions with similar teams within your department on selected performance measures.
- See if other divisions will work with you to sponsor a biannual conference in which teams can showcase significant improvements they've made in selected performance areas.
- Use peers to encourage individuals to consider alternative approaches to their work, as did Gary Blumenthal, president of Tinderbox International, a Los Angeles-based franchisor of tobacco and gift stores:

> Gary Blumenthal . . . has formed a group called The Committee of 90, representing the company's solid performers. The members meet four times a year, discussing various issues and sharing techniques they have tried in their stores. Then Blumenthal assigns them to visit other outlets, where they advise franchises with problems. "It builds a feeling of co-responsibility," he says. "From their peers the advice is both much less threatening and much more embarrassing."[8]

Strategy 2. Challenge the Limits

- **Raise the bar.** This tactic involves raising the bar, that is, setting more difficult performance standards. In a *Fortune* magazine article titled, "Thriving in a Lame Economy," Rahul Jacob stresses the importance of setting high performance targets: "Most managers' instincts are to get cautious in tough times, but many successful executives and consultants advise just the opposite. Set outside targets. Employees must think more boldly, not less, when growth is slow."[9]

In my consulting practice I frequently encounter managers who say that they've made efforts to raise the bar for their teams but have seen few payoffs. Upon closer observation, these failures can always be traced to one of these factors:

- The manager's message that the team must raise its performance level wasn't credible. This manager is like the angry parent who, upon receiving a poor report card from his child, issues vague threats that "this better not happen again," only to forget entirely about the incident until the next time it occurs. The child, knowing the game well, learns to lay low until the entire situation blows over and things return to normal.
- The new performance expectations were unilaterally presented by the manager with no input from the team.

- The new performance standards were too vague or addressed performance factors that were well outside the team's control.
- The team felt that the manager's new performance standards were completely unattainable.
- The manager created consequences that were at odds with desired performance.

To overcome these roadblocks, consider these two steps. First, dramatically raise your expectations on a few key performance measures. Focus your efforts on the vital few performance areas most important to your team's survival. (Challenge 3 discusses how to select outputs that are important to your customers and your manager.)

Second, select performance goals that can be measured. The performance goals you select should include a definitive time frame, focus on discrete performance areas, be quantifiable, and be worded in such a way as to be relatively free from ambiguity. If you aren't sure whether your performance goals meet these criteria, ask your team and a trusted associate to help you troubleshoot them.

- **Close escape hatches.** Whenever you challenge your team to test its performance, you are likely to encounter resistance from some members. Quite frequently this resistance will not be presented directly at the start of a job assignment or project but will begin to emerge subtly only after a work effort is well under way and the performance pressure begins to build. Closing escape hatches means anticipating the types of excuses and rationalizations you are likely to encounter for the team's failure to achieve its goals and eliminating these excuses well before they have an opportunity to delay or derail a project.

One of the best methods for closing escape hatches is to have your team play the role of devil's advocate and for each stage of an anticipated project identify the following:

- The types of problems or roadblocks it is likely to encounter.
- How these roadblocks or problems might affect the success of the project.
- The types of actions that could be taken to prevent these problems from occurring or to get around them after they've occurred. (The *Project Planning Worksheet* in Challenge 3 is a useful tool for helping you lead this discussion.)
- An agreement regarding when and how you will alert each other to changes that could affect progress on a project. (The *Problem Scenario Exercise* in Challenge 1 provides a structured method for facilitating this type of discussion with your team.)

• **Redefine achievable performance.** An important tactic is to encourage members to raise their expectations for their own performance. You may find benchmarking a helpful tool for accomplishing this
perceptual shift. Benchmarking can force members to challenge their
assumptions about the best possible performance that can be expected
within a given area and to identify the best practices that are consistently used by the top performers in a field.

As an example, one step that led to the revitalization of Xerox
was its decision to compare its copiers to those made by its Japanese
competitors. Xerox found that the Japanese companies could produce
copy machines at a much lower cost, even when such factors as labor
costs were taken into consideration.[10]

To apply benchmarking as a motivational tool:

1. Identify an organization that has a function similar to your own
   and that is recognized for having demonstrated world-class
   performance. This function need not be in the same industry
   but should face challenges similar to your own. One of Xerox's
   first benchmarking studies was performed against L. L. Bean, a
   manufacturer of sporting clothes. Xerox selected L. L. Bean for
   study because the two companies' warehousing operations
   faced similar challenges.[11]
2. Clearly determine the criteria that you will use to compare your
   operation with those of the benchmarked organization. If you
   are comparing your performance on delivery schedules, you
   could measure from the point a delivery order is received to
   final delivery or from the time a package leaves your shipping
   dock. Clearly defining your measurement process will keep
   you from attempting to compare apples and oranges during
   your benchmark study.
3. Measure the performance gap between your team's performance and that of the benchmarked organization.
4. Identify those best practices used by the benchmarked organization that could be successfully adopted by your team.
5. Reach agreement with your team regarding the time frame that
   would be required and the improvement actions that would be
   needed in order for your team to close the performance gap.

• **Clone your superstars.** When certain team members consistently outperform others, both the low performers and their managers
sometimes begin to assume that these performance variations are natural, unchangable, and the result of an innate characteristic of the superstars. Nothing could be farther from the truth. One of the most effective

ways of challenging the performance limits that your team has set for itself is by grafting on to your team the skills and competencies of your team's superstars. The following four steps can help you successfully clone your superstars:

1. Measure the gap between the performance of your superstars and your team's average performance level. Some examples are presented in Figure 4-1.
2. Determine whether these performance differences are the result of nonskill-related factors such as:

   - Unique conditions (whether your top sales person was given the most potentially lucrative sales territory)
   - Specialized technical skills that require extensive training (the talented engineer who has specialized training in advanced metallurgical processes)
   - The fact that the top performer has been rewarded differently from other members (receives more attention and coaching from you than do other members)

   If you are able to eliminate these factors, you are safe in assuming that the performance gap is largely the result of skill differences between your top performers and the rest of your team.

3. Break down the performance area under review into discrete activities, and identify areas in which superstars consistently outperform other team members. If you are managing a sales team, you could ask yourself whether the superior performance of certain members results from their approach to cold calling or their method of qualifying sales prospects.

   One word of caution: keep an open mind regarding the best practices for any given activity. I know of a service manager for a car dealership who was surprised to discover that the repair technician with the best record for service call quality and response time actually took much longer than other technicians to initiate repairs. The reason was that the technician spent more time diagnosing a repair problem, resulting in greater overall efficiency in the repair process.

4. Determine the most effective way to transfer these unique skills to your remaining members. Possibilities include:

   - Instituting formal training classes
   - Having top performers lead informal coaching or practice sessions

Figure 4-1. Cloning Superstars.

Function	Performance Gaps	Related Behaviors
Sales	Top two salespeople consistently generate more than 30 percent more sales volume than the team average.	• Territory management • Cold calling • Prospecting • Product demonstrations • Overcoming objections • Closings
Nursing	On a patient survey, one nursing staff member receives a 9.5 rating out of a maximum 10. The average rating for the staff is 5.6.	• Time spent with patients • Responses to patients' questions • Providing information about hospital procedures • How requests are made of the patient (for shots, medication, tests)
Finance	One team member consistently prepares financial statements in less time and with fewer errors and omissions than other members.	• Reconcile current accounts • Consolidate statement from organizational subsidiaries into the corporate accounts • Prepare text calculations • Generate completed financial statements

- Having selected members shadow top performers to observe how to apply certain skills
- Assigning top performers to observe other members and to provide suggestions for improving their performance

- **Model limit-busting in your own life.** If you want your team members to raise their own performance expectations, you must be able to show them you are willing to take risks and challenge performance limits in your own life. James Kouzes and Barry Posner, authors of *The Leadership Challenge: How to Get Extraordinary Things Done in Organizations,* suggest that "the only way leaders can make values tangible and real to followers is through their behaviors and actions. Employees look to their leaders as role models of how they should behave. And when in doubt, they believe actions over words, without fail. . . . Consequently, leaders send signals and messages about which behaviors are appropriate and acceptable and which are not. If leaders ask followers to observe certain standards, then leaders need to live by the same rules."[12]

Living by the same rules means that your team must see that one of the personal values you hold most dear is the importance of continually testing the limits of your own performance. Dane Blumthal, public school teacher, once taught computer, math, and science courses and coached the cross-country team at a small private school. As the result of his efforts, for the first time his team took away top awards at the state level. How could a small private school successfully complete with larger, better-equipped public schools? The answer lay in Dane's unique approach to coaching. He simply ran with his team members, challenging them to keep up with him (he was in his mid-thirties at the time).

On several occasions Dane has been voted Teacher of the Year by his students. The reason is that, like his coaching, his teaching approach is unique. His enthusiasm for his science classes is contagious, because his students see that he still enjoys learning. Over the last few years he's spent his free time helping students build telescopes, perform oceanographic and environmental research, and even construct a communication device that enabled them to monitor an orbiting space satellite. In both his teaching and his coaching, Dane's behavior says to his students, "Life is fascinating. There's a lot to be explored. Let's look further to see what we can find."

To model limit-busting for your team, do the following:

1. Set challenging goals for your performance. During the next month, create a wall chart for tracking your personal performance in a

selected area and include on the chart a clearly delineated performance goal. Share your goal with your team, and be honest in conveying your progress toward the goal. If you find that to reach your goal you have to put in additional effort or modify your procedures, share this with your team. When your team sees that you are testing your own limits, it will be more willing to follow suit.

2. Use the language of success. I've found that the language you use shapes your personal perception of the world. If you use words that convey powerlessness and hopelessness, you weaken yourself. On the other hand, language can be used to empower yourself and strengthen your team. During the next two weeks perform an audit on your communication style and note if any of the self-sabotaging phrases listed in Figure 4-2 creep into your conversation. Listen carefully to yourself to see if you use the language of success or failure. You might also ask someone else to alert you to situations in which you use these phrases.

3. Volunteer to temporarily perform the jobs of your team members. This technique provides a number of benefits. First, it shows employees that you are trying to see through their eyes the problems and difficulties they encounter on a daily basis. Second, if you aren't well acquainted with the jobs they perform, this approach shows that you are willing to shift, when needed, from the role of skilled expert to novice. It shows your team that you are willing to deal with the uncertainty of working outside your comfort zone. An excellent example of this approach was shared with me by Bob Ulevich, division director of operations support for the South Florida Water Management District:

> When I was on special assignment I raffled myself off. We had a lottery for me, complete with lottery tickets. The crews drew from a hat to see who got me for a day. I had to show them that I was willing to commit my time to knowing what they did, and that as a manager I could do this, rather than sit behind a desk. Over a six-month period I did this for about ten work days.[13]

• **Remind your team of its past successes.** During tough times, people become preoccupied with the difficulties they are facing and the setbacks they've experienced. The talk in the hallways and the company cafeteria begins to focus on the big contract that was just lost, rumors of impending layoffs, or the problems created by the latest budget restriction. Sometimes it seems as if nothing is going right in

Figure 4-2. Examples of Self-Sabotaging Phrases.

What we say:	What we mean:
I'm working to the limit of my ability.	I'm topped out. I can't see myself growing stronger or improving my performance. I'm not able to look at innovative ways to improve my job.
As soon as they . . . (senior management, the organization, my manager) take action I'll be able to . . . (make a decision, take action, resolve a problem).	I need direction to function effectively. I respond to others' direction, rather than lead on my own initiative.
What's the use? They probably won't approve it anyway.	What you or I do makes little difference around here. There is no point in giving your best effort.
Eventually I'll get around to that, but I'm just too snowed under now.	There is no way that I can handle everything. I'll resolve things by slipping deadlines.
Just do the best you can. With the staffing situation the way it is, they can't expect miracles.	Given the organizational problems with which we are faced, it's okay to slacken off on your performance standards. I won't be upset if you give less than your best effort.
We just don't have enough information to go on. Why don't we put together a committee for further study?	I can't perform well in a state of ambiguity. I need things painted clearly in black and white before I can act.

the organization. To combat this fatalism and pessimism, it's important for you to provide a vehicle that encourages your team members to focus their attention periodically on what they've done right and on the successes they've achieved in the last few weeks or months. This shift in attention is particularly important when you are first trying to encourage your group to swim upstream against the problems facing them and to tackle initial improvement projects. Bob Stephens, a human resources supervisor in Springfield, Missouri, explains how he helps employees refocus on their successes:

> From time to time we've gone off-site to focus on what we've accomplished in the last six months. We've estab-

lished two ground rules up front for these off-site sessions. First, we devote twenty to thirty minutes to crazy time and allow people to just ventilate their frustrations. I function as the lightening rod in these situations to focus these concerns and issues. This is a tactic used to pop the bubble so that employees can refocus on the topic at hand. Second, we agree to talk about processes, not people. We aren't there to bad-mouth a particular employee or manager, but to work on improving the process.

After ventilating, I ask, "Hey, has anything good happened this past quarter?" We ask people to bring their calendars to the session and comb through them week by week for successes and accomplishments, and we list all of these on flipcharts for review. This enables us to step back and take in the big picture of all of the accomplishments that have been overlooked in the process of attempting to meet our hectic schedules.[14]

• **Create small, incremental successes.** Help your team develop a can-do attitude by generating a series of small incremental successes. James Kouzes and Barry Posner suggest that these types of small wins provide teams with many advantages: wins generate a positive pattern, reduce opposition to change efforts, minimize the fear of failure for members, help build members' confidence, and convey to others that projects are doable within existing skill and resource levels.[15]

James Belasco suggests that managers should "emphasize short-term actions. Management action takes place within a short time-frame perspective. Most managers think and plan thirty to ninety days in advance. . . . Forty-eight hours is the magic time frame. If action isn't taken within forty-eight hours of attendance at a meeting, it will likely never take place. Therefore you want actions that use your vision within forty-eight hours and within thirty to ninety days. . . . Short-term actions create a burst of energy supporting your vision. This energy empowers people."[16]

In *The Breakthrough Strategy* Robert Schaffer talks about the motivational power that's generated by creating breakthrough projects—small-scale, focused projects that provide dramatic performance turnarounds within key performance areas. One example Schaffer discusses is a chemical company that successfully reduced the production cost of a chemical product by focusing on ways to increase the feed rate on its kilns. Another example is the dramatic service improvements achieved by the Bonaventure Express Terminal of the Canadian

National Railway that started when a team agreed to find ways to increase the percentage of shipments that were loaded onto a key train for one important overnight run. In both cases, the initial breakthrough project enabled the participating teams to reevaluate long-held assumptions regarding their ability to make substantial improvements.[17]

The use of small wins and breakthrough projects is especially important when organizations are going through difficult times and teams feel overwhelmed by the changes. Through this tactic teams learn to redirect their energy toward factors that are directly within their scope of control and are better able to buffer themselves against stress.

When selecting a small-scale improvement project for your team, begin by identifying one major performance area that, if improved, would contribute substantially to your organization's success and at the same time make your group feel like a winning team. Schaffer offers the following five guidelines for selecting a breakthrough project:

To ensure success, select a goal that:

1. Is urgent and compelling—a real attention-getter.
2. Is a first-step goal achievable in a short period of time—in weeks rather than months.
3. Is a bottom-line result, discrete and measurable.
4. Is one the responsible participants feel ready, willing, and able to accomplish.
5. Can be achieved with available resources and authority.[18]

After you have selected an area for improvement, the Brainstorming Incremental Improvement Projects in the Tool Kit will provide you with guidelines to assist your team in selecting a small-scale improvement project from this area.

• **Celebrate each success.** It's important to provide ample opportunities to celebrate team successes. Teams suffering from a deficit of positive feedback can quickly become demoralized. Take, for example, the manager of an international sales force whose team was responsible for selling sophisticated computer networks in the domestic, European and Middle East markets. Often the proposal development and review time for these projects stretched out over eighteen months or more. In consulting with the team on steps they could take to improve their performance, I discovered that over time members had been putting less and less energy into their proposals.

According to members, one problem they faced was their manager's insistence that proposal milestones were not causes for celebration. Whenever a milestone was successfully crossed, the manager would quickly remind his team, "This doesn't mean anything until we've won the proposal. It's still early in the bidding process. A lot can happen." What an inspiring speech! It's sort of like standing at the twelve-mile marker of a marathon race and telling a runner, "Don't start feeling optimistic yet. You're only halfway there. You have more than twelve grueling miles to run under the hot sun." Many marathon runners would soon drop out after such a pep talk. Contrast this approach with another possibility:

> Back in 1981 Max Carey, CEO of Corporate Resource Development, Inc., was frustrated by what seemed to him the slow progress of building his Atlanta-based sales and marketing services company. He had just one employee, and "big successes were too far into the future," he says. "There wasn't much to motivate us." His solution? "We decided to celebrate the small interim successes." Carey went out and bought a siren, complete with megaphone and ambulance sound effects. After making a phone sales pitch, he would blow the horn if he had been able to bypass a training director and had reached a CEO. If a big check came in the mail, off went the siren. Now the $1 million-plus company has eleven employees, and the siren goes off about ten times a week. People come out of their offices to hear coworkers brag about their latest achievements, which helps company-wide communications as well. "And it's a great motivator for our less experienced employees," Carey says, "who aren't yet able to produce at top levels."[19]

All teams need frequent celebrations that keep them focused on their goals and help maintain their full level of energy. In Figure 4-3 we provide possible pump-primers. Use them as a starting point for dialoguing with your team members about the types of celebrations they would find meaningful and enjoyable.

Strategy 3: Get Out of the Way

• **Send congruent messages.** After successfully challenging your team's limits, you need to send your team clear signals about the types of performance that you are looking for from them and then get out of their way. This is especially important when the performance expectations for your team are rapidly changing. When the messages you send to your team are unclear, ambiguous, or opaque, the result can be con-

Figure 4-3. Celebrate Each Success.

What should you celebrate?

- Reaching a project milestone
- Overcoming a difficult performance problem
- Catching a problem before it becomes too big
- Surviving a difficult period of organizational change
- Taking on a new responsibility or expanding your team charter
- Adding new members
- Kicking off a major project

How can you celebrate?

Especially if budget cuts and work overload make fancy off-site celebrations impossible!

- Invite members to meet socially after work
- Post success milestones (green flags on a milestone board) where everyone can see them
- Ask your company newspaper to write an article on one of your team's successes
- Invite your entire team to meet with your customers during an on-site visit (if the success involved meeting customer requirements)
- Invite a senior manager to meet with your team and provide a word of thanks or congratulations
- Bring donuts and coffee into one of your team meetings
- Order a humorous plaque for your team
- Have one of your team's lunches catered (order in pizza or sandwiches)
- Check into the possibility of having a team achievement written up in a professional journal or presented by your team at a professional conference or workshop

Reprinted with permission from the PCS Team Development Program, 1989, published and marketed by Parry Consulting Services, Inc.

fusion, anxiety, and inefficiency. Through interviews conducted with 260 managers and employees, Kathleen Ryan and Daniel Oestreich, authors of *Driving Fear Out of the Workplace,* identified ambiguous behavior by managers and supervisors as one of the chief causes of fear and tension in the workplace.[20] Ambiguous management behavior can take a number of forms:

- Formally establishing quality improvement as your highest priority and then allowing wide fluctuations in quality standards to accommodate production pressures
- Telling team members to take greater initiative and then slapping their hands the first time they overstep the invisible boundaries of their job descriptions
- Giving a pep talk in which you encourage members to confront problems honestly and to surface improvement opportunities and then publicly chastising a member for daring to challenge the efficiency of a procedure that you've put into place
- Stating that risk taking will be rewarded and then giving poor evaluations to employees who fail more often because they attempt to do more for the team, while rewarding employees who experience fewer failures simply because they lay low and accomplish little of value

If you discover that your team is having trouble interpreting your behavior, you need to act quickly to correct the situation. A reasonable starting point is to pay attention to those subtle clues that indicate that your members are having difficulty interpreting your behavior, such as the following kinds of behavior:

- Members hesitate to act on the decisions you've put into place or drag their feet in the completion of assignments.
- Members frequently check with you for direction before going further. They have a need for confirmation and approval.
- Members have difficulty sorting out priorities.
- Members commit errors and do rework that could be traced to difficulties in interpreting directions.

Ryan and Oestreich provide a number of suggestions for reducing ambiguous behavior, including providing employees with clear and accurate information, asking people to point out mixed messages that they receive from you, involving people in decisions, and not putting people in double-bind situations that "demand that a person act in a certain way while simultaneously creating barriers to behaving in that way."[21]

• **Create consequences that support desired performance.** Make certain that the performance consequences you've put in place support the types of behavior you are trying to encourage from your team. Consider the following examples:

Delta Audio-Visual Security, Inc., is a New Orleans-based company that sells alarm systems. Bill Bozeman, its CEO, realized that salespeople who work for a fixed-rate commission sometimes tend to focus on their current customers at the cost of generating new prospects, so he came up with the idea of providing his sales team with an extra 1 percent commission on top of its normal commission rate whenever it sells to new customers. As a result, new customer sales rose from 25 to 35 percent over two years.[22]

When G.O.D., Inc., an overnight express freight service, switched from an hourly wage system to a system of paying freight dock workers by the number of shipments they handled, it experienced a tremendous increase in problems related to breakage and freight loss. To counter this, the company changed its reward system. "On top of the shipment rate, freight loaders get weekly bonuses of 25 percent of their total week's earnings if all shipments go through with no breakage, misloading, or short cartons."[23]

These examples illustrate what happens when incentive systems are linked to desired performance. To examine the performance consequences that you've put into place for your team, take the following steps:

1. Identify an area in which you are not getting the type of performance you want from your team. Be specific. Examples might include:

    • Our team's response time for processing new admissions to our hospital
    • The quality defects we are encountering in the finishing stage of production runs
    • Our ability to respond politely and completely to requests for information from other departments
    • Our excessive time to completion for new project bids
    • Our difficulty in increasing the number of new accounts we are generating each month

2. Now briefly describe the types of behavior that would support superior performance in the selected area. For example, if the area is "our ability to respond politely and completely to requests for information from other departments," desired behavior might include such things as:

    • Staying on the line until a problem is resolved
    • Providing complete information to your internal customers
    • Politely explaining to customers why certain requests for assistance can't be met

3. Now contrast this ideal behavior with the behavior you are currently getting from members:

- Being rude or abrupt on the phone
- Providing minimal responses ("No, we can't do that") that don't explain why certain requests can't be met
- A tendency for individuals to pass on requests for assistance to other members rather than tracking down information or attempting to answer difficult technical questions raised by customers

4. Ask yourself the following questions:
   - What consequences support desired behavior? What positive things happen when members do it right?
   - What consequences actually discourage desired behavior? What punishing things happen when members do it right?
   - What consequences support undesired behavior? In what ways are members rewarded when they do it wrong?
   - What consequences discourage undesired behavior? What punishing things happen when members perform poorly?

Many managers are skeptical that such a simple line of inquiry can produce any information of value. The trick is to consider all possible performance consequences from the point of view of your members.

For example, members may appear unresponsive to customers' inquiries or requests for assistance for very different reasons. Members may not mind occasionally being criticized for being rude to customers on the phone if they know a large part of their performance evaluation is based on how fast they respond to customers. Consequently, they may rush through phone inquiries, cut off customers in the middle of discussion, or be overly abrupt in their responses. Another explanation may be that members are afraid of giving the wrong answers to customers because they lack necessary information or because they feel that you are very controlling about the types of information given out by your team.

Over the next week, take a look at the performance consequences that you've put in place for your team. Keep in mind that whenever you make major changes in your performance expectations, you have to follow suit with corresponding changes to your performance consequences. Finally, test your assumptions against input provided from your members or other managers who have seen you interact with your team. Try to remain open to their suggestions, even if it means changing your management style.

- **Empower strategically.** In Challenge 1 I discussed the importance of team empowerment in enabling your team to respond quickly to changing conditions. Empowerment also plays a critical role in encouraging your team to give its full effort and commitment. At this point you are probably thinking, "Sounds good, but given the difficult work situation we are encountering I don't feel very comfortable about just turning over a lot of authority to my team. After all, at this point our performance is being watched very carefully, and I can't afford major mistakes." I agree with you completely. On the other hand, can you afford to have your team working at less than 50 percent efficiency because it lacks the authority to make effective decisions or to respond to your customers in a timely fashion? The question is how to balance your need for minimizing risks with the need for increasing team efficiency. The answer is use strategic empowerment—matching empowerment to the competency level of each member.

First consider that true empowerment is dependent on both *empowering* actions and *enabling* actions. Empowering actions are those that provide individuals with additional autonomy over their work. Enabling actions are those management actions that prepare individuals to make effective use of this new authority, by helping them develop the skills, competencies, and knowledge they need to take over greater responsibilities.

In the best of all possible worlds enablement and empowerment are in perfect balance. In real life they are often out of sync. Strategic empowerment means determining each member's needs with respect to empowerment and enablement and providing the support, coaching, instruction, and/or authority needed for the individual to best perform the job. Members can be classified into one of four categories, depending on the degree to which they are empowered and enabled.

1. *Entrenched bunkers*—members who are powerless and lack the skills needed to perform their jobs effectively. Feeling completely overwhelmed by their jobs, these individuals often respond either by becoming 'invisible' and focusing on responsibilities that lie in the center of their comfort zone or by becoming very dependent on other members (and on you, their manager) for support and direction. For these individuals, strategic empowerment requires the following steps:

- Set up clear performance measures and encourage the individual to track her performance against these measures.
- Set up a meeting to review the individual's performance. Be prepared that the individual may ask you to bail him out by attempting to shift responsibilities to other members or by asking you to provide him with an excessive amount of hand-holding. Clearly outline the performance standards you expect this individual to meet and explain that he will be held accountable.

- Explain that you will provide support in the form of assisting her in developing needed skills.
- Don't overwhelm them by outlining all of their skill deficiencies. Instead, reach agreement on those few skills deficiencies that are creating the greatest problems for the individual on the job.
- Discuss alternatives for building required skills. If your own time is extremely limited, ask a competent team member to provide additional coaching.
- Set up a time for a follow-up discussion on the individual's progress on her skill development plans.

2. *Loose cannons*—individuals who have been given (or falsely assume they have) a broad degree of control over their jobs, even though their low competence level causes them to experience performance problems. These individuals cause senior managers to add additional controls and check points. Strategically empower loose cannons through the following steps:

- Prior to your meeting, identify performance problems that have previously occurred because the member attempted to take actions that were beyond her skill level. Try to pinpoint the primary gaps between this individual's competence level and the degree of independent action and authority she exhibits.
- Review these situations with the member. Ask the member to summarize how he views his performance in each situation and the actions that could have been taken to avoid these situations; then provide your feedback. Be prepared to encounter some resistance; the member is likely to provide a number of excuses for his problems and attempt to draw attention away from his skill deficiencies.
- Outline your performance expectations and clearly explain areas in which you feel the individual may be deficient.
- Discuss alternatives for building needed skills. If your own time is extremely limited, ask a competent member to serve as a coach to assist the member.
- At the same time, discuss putting in temporary safeguards to prevent additional performance problems during the skill-building process, such as teaming the individual with another, more competent employee; limiting the member's decision-making authority until she has successfully demonstrated skill growth; and clearly identifying check-in points at which the member will receive work review and coaching.

- Discuss a time for a follow-up discussion on the individual's progress toward meeting her skill development goals.

3. *Caged eagles*—individuals who lack the authority and autonomy they need to make effective use of their skills and experience. They are often underutilized in the organization and represent a potential waste of human resources. Take the following two steps to strategically empower these members:

First, ask the member to come to the meeting prepared to discuss representative situations in which he has had difficulty performing his work because of his lack of authority. Perhaps the member:

- Was not permitted to pass on information to other groups
- Had to wait for your approval to make routine decisions
- Lacks sign-off authority for documentation that is an important part of her job
- Is not permitted the flexibility of creating her own schedule or selecting her own work methods

During this conversation, listen nondefensively to the member and remain open to critical feedback concerning your management style. Next, discuss options for shifting additional authority over to the member, while minimizing unnecessary risks. Look for an option that will serve as a brief and timely mini-experiment for testing the individual's ability to handle additional responsibility.

4. *Fully empowered*—workers with both the competence and the authority they need to achieve top performance. They are operating close to their maximum performance level and usually make the greatest contribution to your team. When working with such an individual, you should:

- Periodically meet to look for opportunities to broaden and extend her contribution to your team
- Make certain you've removed all empowerment roadblocks that could hamper her performance
- Consider work experiences that would enable him to serve as a successful role model for other members

It's sometimes difficult to determine where employees fit into this two-dimensional empowerment model, because both employees' skill levels and work conditions can change rapidly over time. For this reason, you may want to make use of the Empowerment Profile in the Tool Kit. This simple ten-statement survey can provide you with accurate feedback on how employees view their competence levels and their degree of empowerment.

TOOL KIT

Crystal Ball Exercise

This exercise requires input from your entire team and takes approximately one hour. It is designed to help your team members understand how they may need to adapt and strengthen their performance to address changing organizational requirements.

1. Prior to your team meeting, draw on a flipchart an empty crystal ball. On a second flipchart sheet, draw a similar crystal ball incorporating the comments in Figure 4-4.
2. Introduce the exercise in your own words. For example: "As you all know, our company is going through changes that will significantly affect the role we play in supporting our company's business goals and performance expectations. Over the next hour we will be using this empty crystal ball to identify those changes that you feel are likely to make the biggest im-

Figure 4-4.   Crystal ball exercise.

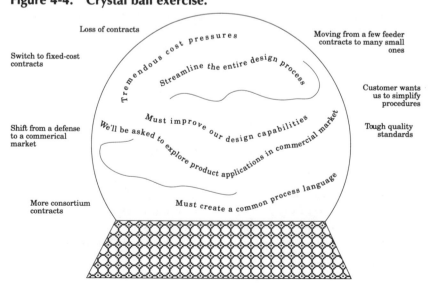

pact on our organization and to record your suggestions for how we can best prepare ourselves to meet these changes."

3. Ask team members to draw similar crystal balls on their papers, and give them five minutes to write in the space outside their circles up to three major changes that are either currently taking place in your organization or are likely to occur over the next two years. To prime the pump, share with your team the examples provided in Figure 4-4.

4. Give participants another five minutes to describe inside the circle how they feel your team will need to adapt its performance to meet these organizational changes. Suggest that they use arrows to show the connections between organizational changes and changing performance demands. Explain that an organizational change can require a variety of adaptive responses from your team. Again, share the examples provided in Figure 4-4.

5. Ask a member to write her responses on the flipchart and to summarize them. Invite other members to build on this drawing. Have each member complete this step and continue to revise and embellish the flipchart drawing.

6. When all members have provided their input, add your own suggestions to the flipchart drawing.

7. Ask several members to summarize their conclusions from the exercise.

8. Ask participants to help you rate the relative importance of each performance challenge that they've identified.

This exercise can help your team gain perspective on the increasing performance demands it is likely to face during the next two years. You may want to keep this list available for use whenever you need to explain to your team the need for implementing difficult improvement projects.

Brainstorming Incremental Improvement Projects

This discussion involves all your team members and takes approximately two to four hours. It can be used to introduce your team to changing performance standards and to obtain their suggestions for how to implement performance improvement projects.

1. Prior to the meeting, identify one key area in which you would like to see your team improve its performance.

2. Meet with your members and explain that you are asking them to take on the challenge of improving the team's performance in the area you've selected. Be prepared to encounter resistance from some individuals, but stand firm in explaining that you consider this performance area to be a top priority for your team. Explain that the purpose of the meeting is to reach agreement on actions that your team could take to improve its performance in this area.

3. Ask your team to help you break down the selected performance area into its component activities.

4. Identify those activities that, if improved, could contribute significantly to the overall performance of the area under review.

5. If necessary, break down the activity into major tasks and again select one task for the review.

6. Ask your team to help you identify projects that could be used for improving its performance in the selected tasks or activities. Give members five minutes to generate privately some ideas for improvement projects.

7. While your team is engaged in Step 6, draw on the board the Improvement Options Map (Challenge 3). Explain the purpose of this map and say that you are trying to look for projects that fall into the "Sprint" category. You will consider marathon projects but will require that your team help you break them into bite size chunks.

There is a tendency for individuals to underestimate the degree of control they have over an improvement area. If you find that participants are paying too much attention to factors they consider to be outside their control, challenge them to look for ways to convert these uncontrollables into controllables. For example, if team members say that one factor contributing to bottlenecks in a documentation process is the delay they encounter in receiving information from another department (an uncontrollable factor), ask them to identify actions they could take to encourage the department to meet agreed-upon delivery schedules. These (controllable) steps might include:

- Setting up a supplier/customer contracting session
- Making it easier for the other team to provide this information (by simplifying documentation forms or providing clerical assistance)
- Delivering friendly reminders to the other team whenever they begin to fall behind schedule

8. Create a detailed plan outlining the first steps members will take during the next two to four weeks to implement their selected improvement actions. The Project Planning Worksheet (Challenge 3) may be helpful in this step.
9. Agree on a date for a follow-up discussion.

Empowerment Profile

The Empowerment Profile (Figure 4-5) is designed to enable you and your team members to compare views on the degree to which members have both the skills and the information (enablement) and the authority and autonomy (empowerment) they need to perform their work.

The profile consists of ten statements, five of which pertain to empowerment and five of which pertain to enablement. Respondents are asked to rate their level of agreement with each statement on a scale of 1 to 5, so the total for a dimension can range from 5 to 25. Using these scores, members can identify which of the four types they fit in to. For example, in Figure 4-6 a member having a score of 19 for empowerment and an 8 for enablement would be a Loose Cannon; someone with a score of 5 for empowerment and a 7 for enablement would be an Entrenched Bunker.

You should also complete an Empowerment Profile for the member under review by answering each statement from your point of view. Later, you can compare your scores with his. This comparison can be very useful in identifying perception gaps that may be contributing to performance problems. By administering the profile to several members, you can also begin to look for scoring patterns that can help you leverage the performance of your entire team.

Notes

1. John Huey, "Where Will the Managers Go?" *Fortune* (January 27, 1992), pp. 50–58. © 1992, Time Inc. All rights reserved.
2. Interview with Patrick Miller, director of human resources for TECO Transport and Trade, May 1993.
3. Robert H. Schaffer, "Breakthrough Project Selection Guidelines," in *The Breakthrough Strategy: Using Short-Term Successes to Build the High-Performance Organization* (Cambridge, Mass.: Ballinger, 1988), p. 63. Reprinted by permission of HarperCollins Publishers, Inc.

Figure 4-5. The Empowerment Profile.

Profile Instructions: Rate your level of agreement with each statement using a 1-to-5 scale, 5 being complete agreement and 1 complete disagreement. Total your scores for each dimension. Your manager will show you how to interpret your scores.

Name: _____

Date: _____

Empowerment Dimension

____ 1. I have access to the information I need (objectives, financial statements, production runs, quality defect reports) to do my work effectively.

____ 2. I am given opportunities to provide input on important team decisions.

____ 3. I am allowed to self-manage my work (adjust my schedule and work methods) as I see fit.

____ 4. I am able to work directly with my team's internal or external customers and suppliers.

____ 5. I am encouraged to take the initiative to uncover problems or make improvements.

____ Dimension Total (min. score 5; max. 25)

Enablement Dimension

____ 1. I know how to interpret information (objectives, financial statements, production runs, quality defect reports) that is important to the performance of my job.

____ 2. I have the decision-making skills needed to provide input on important team decisions.

____ 3. I know how to self-manage my work (planning schedule, managing time, selecting effective work methods).

____ 4. I have the skills needed to answer questions from, negotiate with, or resolve problems with our team's internal or external customers and suppliers.

____ 5. I have the skills needed to resolve problems and make improvements.

____ Dimension Total (min. score 5; max. 25)

Figure 4-6. Empowerment Profile Ratings.

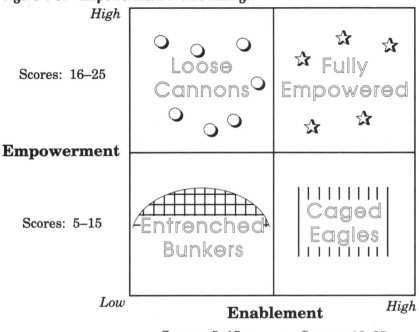

From Robert Barner, "Enablement: The Flip Side of Empowerment," *Training and Development Journal* (June 1994). Copyright 1994, the American Society for Training and Development. Reprinted with permission.

4. James Belasco, *Teaching the Elephant to Dance: The Manager's Guide to Empowering Change* (New York: Crown, 1991), p. 20.
5. Judith M. Bardwick, *Danger in the Comfort Zone: From Boardroom to Mailroom—How to Break the Entitlement Habit That's Killing American Business* (New York: AMACOM, 1991), p.77. Reprinted with permission of the publisher. © 1991 Judith M. Bardwick, Ph.D.
6. David Sanger, "Japan's Supercars: Cheaper and Better," *Palm Beach Post Times* (January 6, 1990).
7. Bardwick, *Danger in the Comfort Zone*, p.93.
8. Sara P. Noble, ed., *301 Great Management Ideas from America's Most Innovative Small Companies* (Boston: Goldhirsh Group, 1991), p. 1. Reprinted with permission, *Inc.* magazine, 1991. ©1991 by Goldhirsh Group, Inc., 38 Commercial Wharf, Boston, MA 02110.
9. Rahul Jacob, "Thriving in a Lame Economy," *Fortune* (October 5, 1992), pp. 44–54. © 1992 Time Inc. All rights reserved.

10. Marion Harmon, "Benchmarking," *Quality Digest* (July 1992), pp. 20–31.
11. Harmon, "Benchmarking," pp. 20–31.
12. James M. Kouzes and Barry Z. Posner, *The Leadership Challenge: How to Get Extraordinary Things Done in Organizations* (San Francisco: Jossey-Bass, 1987), pp. 198–199. ©1987 by Jossey-Bass, Inc., Publishers.
13. Interview with Bob Ulevich, division director of operations support for the South Florida Water Management District, June 1993.
14. Interview with Bob Stephens, human resources supervisor, 3M of Springfield, Missouri, June 1993.
15. Kouzes and Posner, *The Leadership Challenge*, pp. 220–222.
16. Belasco, *Teaching the Elephant to Dance*, pp. 141–142.
17. Robert H. Schaffer, "Breakthrough Project Selection Guidelines," p. 63.
18. Ibid., p. 64.
19. Noble, *301 Great Management Ideas*, p. 60.
20. Kathleen D. Ryan and Daniel K. Oestreich, *Driving Fear Out of the Workplace* (San Francisco: Jossey-Bass, 1991), p. 76.
21. Ryan and Oestreich, *Driving Fear Out of the Workplace*, p. 181.
22. Noble, *301 Great Management Ideas*, p. 91.
23. Noble, *301 Great Management Ideas*, p. 99.

Challenge 5

Close Ranks and Reform

Inadequate or Excess Staff

If your organization is encountering disruptive changes, you may find it difficult to forecast accurately your requirements and to balance your workload against your available staff. You may find yourself in one of two diametrically opposed situations.

First, you may not have the staff you need to perform the required work. This challenge can be especially problematic if your workload is rapidly increasing, your team is expanding into entirely new responsibilities, or you have recently lost several members. In all these situations, you will need to determine how to reorganize your staff to meet your objectives. Moreover, if your organization is encountering tough times, you will find it difficult to convince your managers to add additional full-time staff. You may even be operating within an organization that considers personnel reductions a convenient answer to the problem of soaring costs.

Understaffed teams encounter a number of performance challenges. They usually have greater difficulty meeting their objectives and experience excessive stress and overload from the pressure of working without adequate resources. These factors adversely affect work quality as teams scramble to meet impossible deadlines and work pressures.

On the other hand, you may find yourself with excess staff. I know it sounds a bit strange to target excess staff as a management problem, but consider the implications. When groups have little to do, their attention shifts toward petty frustrations. As members begin to intrude on each other's work and coordination becomes more difficult, complaints increase and operations become less efficient. In addition, if your group doesn't see itself as productive, members will quickly become demoralized. More important, if your team is sitting idle, eventually someone is going to question the cost of supporting your staff, increasing the chances that your members will be transferred, laid off, or subject to staffing raids by other managers. Finally, others will seriously question your ability to manage your resources effectively.

A reason for the success of the Roman legions was their ability to respond quickly to threats by closing ranks and reforming into new positions. If a soldier went down, the ranks closed to fill the gap. If the legions were suddenly met with a shower of stones or arrows, shields were uniformly raised to form a protective cover. If the enemy shifted its attack, at a single command the legions suddenly regrouped into specialized formations specifically designed to counter those attacks. In much the same way, the answer to the staffing challenges you are facing lies in knowing how to close ranks effectively and reform your troops.

In this chapter you will be introduced to the strategies, tactics, and tools you need to match your responsibilities effectively to your group's skills and experience. We discuss how to assess your staffing problems, uncover alternative resources to accomplish your work, and reposition members to prevent unnecessary staff reductions. In addition, we explain how to leverage available staff and obtain the best possible performance with the resources you have available.

Warning Symptoms

Perhaps you haven't encountered this challenge but are concerned that it may be rapidly approaching. Use the following symptoms index to determine the importance of this challenge to your team.

Symptoms of Insufficient Staff

❑ Your team is about to take on a major responsibility that is outside its experience and training.

❑ You are finding it necessary to take over more and more of your team's responsibilities in an effort to help members keep up with their workloads.

❑ Stress, overtime, and work overload are increasing, and team members appear fatigued and overwhelmed.

❑ Schedule deadlines are being postponed or are frequently missed.

❑ It's becoming harder to track all your group's job assignments and responsibilities. Work falls between the cracks as members haphazardly jump from job to job.

Symptoms of Excess Staff

- ❏ An organization-wide headcount study has indicated that you have far more resources than other, similar groups in your company.

- ❏ You've been pressured by senior managers to identify those members whom you consider replaceable or to rate a certain percentage of members as poor performers.

- ❏ Other managers are attempting to conduct staffing raids on your team to beef up their own groups.

- ❏ Many members of your group are sitting idle.

- ❏ Members are becoming more territorial and are vying for control of each others' responsibilities.

Strategies

If you believe you have insufficient staff to meet your responsibilities, start by determining whether your team has the bench strength needed to meet changing responsibilities and address emerging job challenges. This strategy provides you with the baseline information you need to determine the severity of your staffing problem and to identify the most effective solutions to this problem. If your level of staffing is in fact inadequate, it's wise to take steps to increase the productivity of your existing staff before attempting to obtain additional staff. You can also seek surrogate help, including student interns, volunteers, assistants, and "imports" from other departments. You need to weigh the pros and cons associated with each option and select the staffing solution that best meets your overall needs.

If you are faced with excess staff, consider redirecting your staff to special projects or assignments within or outside your group. Never assume that your managers fully understand the bottom-line impact of reducing your staff. Prepare reasonable arguments to show that arbitrary or excessive staff cuts could seriously reduce your team's performance and identify alternatives for generating needed cost reductions.

If you are faced with the need to reduce staff, explore ways to minimize the impact of staff reductions through alternative staff transition plans, such as job sharing or rotational layoffs.

Strategies and Tactics for Insufficient Staff

Strategy 1: Evaluate Your Human Resources Capabilities

• **Inventory team responsibilities.** Inventory the responsibilities and projects performed by your team to determine whether each area is receiving adequate coverage. This tactic can help you identify the best way to meet actual or potential staff reductions, work around temporary staff reassignments, provide developmental assignments to members, or identify ways to gradually build up the self-management skills of the team. The Team Transition Chart in the Tool Kit is excellent for generating this inventory.

• **Benchmark your team's strength.** If you are concerned about not having the skills and experience required to handle emerging responsibilities, talk to others who have been there. Begin with your manager, and obtain as much information as you can about any new functions your team is likely to assume during the coming year. Then use your professional network to identify other organizations' teams that have successfully taken on similar responsibilities. Obtain these teams' recommendations regarding:

- The types of technical skills and experience required to successfully manage these responsibilities
- Areas in which your team lacks the bench strength to manage these responsibilities
- Steps your members can take to develop quickly the required skills

I know of a counseling firm that interviewed noncompetitive service agencies regarding the skills its employees would need in order to wade successfully through the federal procurement and proposal process. The Team Benchmarking Chart in the Tool Kit may be helpful as you perform this benchmarking.

Strategy 2: Leverage Available Staff

• **Unload ballast.** Look for ways to lighten your workload by getting rid of unnecessary work. A good starting point is to use the Performance Map (in Challenge 3's Tool Kit) to determine the relative importance of your outputs. Look into the feasibility of eliminating outputs that don't add significant value to your customers. If this is impossible, see if these outputs can be performed less frequently, in less time, or in a more bare-bones manner. Focus your staff and your energy on those few outputs that are most important to your customers.

• **Automate labor-intensive activities.** Try to find ways to automate all time-consuming and paper-intensive activities. Perhaps you could provide sales agents with laptop computers and spreadsheet software to reduce the time spent in maintaining expense records, or perhaps your existing software could be updated to reduce the number of keystrokes required for repetitive, labor-intensive data inputting.

• **Consolidate responsibilities.** Are there other departments or divisions of your company that are performing responsibilities similar to your own? Could these responsibilities be shared on a rotating basis or consolidated under one area for increased productivity? For example, Terry Geraghty, director of organizational development for Harris Electronic Systems Sector, provided his organization with a cost/benefit study that showed that within his organization it was much more effective to consolidate all educational assistance at the sector level than to have each sector's divisions attempt to assign a staff member to manage this function on a part-time basis.[1]

• **Use incentives to balance staff with workloads.** If you don't have sufficient staff to handle peak work periods such as evening hours, rush hours, or seasonal requirements, consider offering financial incentives to encourage members to make needed adjustments to their workloads. First National Bank of Chicago substantially reduced waiting time in its teller lines by creating an incentive program for tellers that enables them to earn a higher rate of pay during peak times, such as lunch hours and holidays.[2] If you don't have the option of providing financial incentives, consider giving volunteers compensatory time off or priority in attending off-site seminars or selecting vacation periods.

• **Transfer responsibilities to other departments.** If you feel that you are going to be permanently understaffed and won't be able to manage everything, try transferring some responsibilities to other departments. One simple way of getting your entire team to help you identify transferable functions is by completing the Bull's-eye Exercise in the Tool Kit.

• **Have customers perform their own work.** A related tactic is to train your internal customers to perform some of the work that you currently provide for them. While managers argue that taking this action will make them less valuable to their organization, keep in mind that by enabling your internal customers to perform some of your routine and time-consuming work, you enable your staff to focus on more difficult and challenging projects.

One manager who uses this tactic is Brian Chitester, a director of process improvement for Pepsi Cola, whose team is responsible for helping six company divisions establish process improvement programs. He provides the following explanation of his team's approach to their customers:

> What we've been doing is contracting up-front with our customers regarding what the process is, the identification of the team's improvement goals, who at the facility will be held accountable for results, and the type of support our team will provide. We write into the contract that there will be a weaning-away process during the first four to six weeks, and after that it's up to our customers to establish the capability to take over the job.[3]

The Customer Interview Guidelines discussed in the Tool Kit for Challenge 3 can help you gather information when negotiating with your customers for the transfer of job responsibilities.

Strategy 3: Obtain Surrogate Help

• **Lease/contract temporary help.** If your team experiences brief periods of high-volume activity, consider leasing help to get you through those periods. For years retail stores have hired temporaries to help them through the holiday season or during inventories. Since the 1980s the temporary field has mushroomed to include such professionals as engineers, accountants, and systems analysts, and many skilled professionals can now be obtained through temporary services. One of our clients frequently leases an extra accountant during November and December to help his company finalize its end-of-year financial closings. I know of a company whose personnel department hired a recruiter on a contract basis to help it quickly bring on board additional staff to expand one of its international facilities.

At the other extreme, you can hire a contract employee to perform some of the most routine and time-consuming work performed by your group. This option becomes particularly attractive if you are dealing with certain tasks that are largely self-contained (e.g., data inputting) and that do not require a high level of coordination with other activities.

• **Use assistants as an option to professional staff.** I frequently hear managers screaming for additional professional staff when they actually don't need them. A classic example is that of engineers who spend a large part of their time on document preparation or data inputting, tasks that could just as easily be performed by aides. Other examples are lawyers who perform work that could be undertaken by paralegals and human resources professionals who perform tasks that could be managed by personnel assistants.

The tactic of obtaining assistants to free up professionals' time for value-added activities is used by many of the top-producing life insurance agents. These agents frequently hire assistants to handle all their administrative and paperwork activities so that they can devote their time to sales activities.[4]

As a first step in pursuing this tactic, use the Team Transition Chart in your Tool Kit to distinguish between those activities that require a high level of expertise and those that could be performed by an assistant.

• **Create a college intern program.** Another useful tactic is to explore with your local college the option of bringing on board a student intern. If no such program exists, why not create one? Sometimes by offering to pay for meals, local travel expenses, and, in some cases, a small stipend, you can obtain excellent help. Years ago I used this tactic when I was employed as a correctional rehabilitation counselor with a state agency. Lacking adequate staff, I faced the challenge of finding the time to connect agency clients to state and community support agencies. I contacted a local university and created a program that provided hands-on experience for university students who assisted me in coordinating activities with local social service agencies.

The city of Lakeland, Florida, uses college interns to supplement its staff. Jane Rose, the city's training manager, says that one of the keys to a successful internship program is to provide participating universities with a list of what the job entails and the courses that students should complete before beginning their internships. In addition, if an organization relies on one university for students, that university and its students will develop a better understanding of what the hiring organization requires of its interns. Still another suggestion offered by Jane is to design the intern program to provide a one-week overlap between students who are completing internship assignments and those who are just coming on board so that experienced interns can help orient new students to their assignments.[5]

• **Link employees' educational goals to your projects.** If some of your company's employees are involved in college degree programs, why not give them the option of linking these program requirements to your work requirements? For example, several of AT&T Paradyne's employees attend Eckerd College, which offers nontraditional degree programs. Mark Johnson, manager of quality curriculum for AT&T Paradyne, says, "Rather than have these employees write a research paper on some abstract subject, we are beginning to help them select an assignment within the company that shows clear evidence of their skills in the workplace, as well as fulfilling work requirements."[6]

• **Use volunteers.** If you work in a nonprofit organization, consider the possibility of developing a volunteer program. The Supplemental Staff Questionnaire in the Tool Kit lists some of the most important questions you need to address before bringing on board volunteers, student interns, or loaned employees from other departments.

• **Obtain services through local community agencies.** Some of the work that your team currently performs or would like to perform might be available at no cost through local community agencies. Years ago, I was given the job of setting up a remedial skills program to help employees develop basic reading, writing, and math skills. Through my professional network I heard about a local technical training center that provided these services through a grant-funded program it had recently initiated. The center was able to set up an on-site remedial skills program for our employees, at no cost to our company. Our company provided the training facility, while the agency provided the staff and necessary teaching materials. As a by-product of this effort, once the learning center was established we began to introduce computer-based remedial training. Eventually, this enabled us to develop the core facilities we needed to establish a full-scale, self-directed learning center at little cost to our company.

Many country and state agencies now provide special business counseling services to companies certified as women-owned or minority-owned and to small businesses. These services may include special educational programs on how to do business with government agencies, bid on proposals, or manage financial accounts. If your organization falls into one of these categories, contact your appropriate government agencies to find out how you can become certified and learn about any business support services these agencies provide.

• **Trade/borrow help from other departments.** If your group's workload suffers from feast-and-famine cycles, contact another person or group that is in a similar situation to explore the possibility of loaning each other staff. Sometimes employees are eager to take on this type of job rotation assignment because it helps them broaden their skill base and offers a break in their work routine. A simple technique for accomplishing this exchange is to create a time line with the other manager. Indicate the times during the next few months when each of you anticipates encountering heavy workloads and the types of assistance required during these periods.

The human resources department of Harris Corporation has had many line professionals take on HR assignments as part of its professional development plans. Terry Geraghty, director of organizational development for Harris Electronic Systems Sector, says that a key selling point for enlisting volunteers is to show departments that these assignments will provide greater involvement with and input into the design of the process. Another key to success is to be precise in communicating performance expectations. For example, you might ask a volunteer to take a prototype of a performance planning system, review it with colleagues, troubleshoot it, propose suggestions for revision, and determine how the system could be most effectively communicated to the general population.[7]

• **Ask your internal customers for assistance.** Develop documentation showing your internal customers how the use of additional staff could help you provide them with faster turn-around for their work or would enable you to provide services that you can't currently provide. Then see if they are willing to loan you staff or help pay for the cost of obtaining new staff.

• **Be your own contractor.** Examine the possibility of bidding out routine job functions to all company employees on an after-hours contract basis. This was the tactic used by Erie Bolt Corporation, which decided to allow its employees to bid on janitorial services. It found that its own employees underbid an outside contractor and also provided better service.[8] Another company supplements its sales efforts by providing all nonsales personnel with bonuses of up to one thousand dollars for passing along the names of prospective customers to the sales force.[9]

The city of Lakeland, Florida, invites its employees to volunteer to take on part-time, after-hours work providing phone coverage during electric power outages. Employees can come from any position and receive a flat pay rate. All volunteers receive training in how to handle customers and are brought in as needed. Jane Rose, the city's training director, says that one advantage of this arrangement is that employees learn a lot more about their organization; another is that it provides a good team-building process that gets people from different departments to work together. In addition, the city knows that the people who are manning the phones during power outages are motivated volunteers who have asked to take on the job. Jane says that an additional advantage of this arrangement is that it relieves the stress of the full-time customer service representatives, many of whom are parents who don't want to work evenings.[10]

• **Inventory employees' skills.** During tough times, managers tend to hoard staff for fear of being forced to give up members to other groups, thereby weakening their own power base in the organization. Unfortunately, this process tends to bring on feast-and-famine cycles within those departments, with some groups understaffed and others overstaffed. One of the most effective methods of preventing the hoarding of staff is to suggest to your manager that your department put together a skill inventory, mapping out the technical skill competencies of each team.

A small electronics plant successfully adapted a version of this tactic by asking its employees to complete a survey in which they were asked to list special skills, abilities, or hobbies. The company then gave these employees recognition by devoting a series of articles in the company newspaper to some of the more interesting entries. The survey also enabled the plant to locate employees who could be used on special job assignments or who might be eligible for other positions. For example, Bob Stephens, the human resources supervisor who helped implement this project, was asked to put together a marketing brochure after the marketing department discovered he had a background in journalism. One of the company's manufacturing operators obtained a position in the company's engineering department after the survey revealed that the employee had extensive experience in drafting and mechanical drawing. To jump-start a 3M facility's annual United Way drive, the plant used a survey to locate employees who had previously worked as volunteers with United Way agencies or whose families had used the services of those agencies. The efforts of these employee volunteers resulted in a 12 percent increase in employee contributions, surpassing the contribution levels for many other 3M facilities.[11]

• **Jointly review your organization's succession plans.** If your company uses a succession planning system for targeting emerging talent, ask your senior managers to consider conducting a joint review of succession plan candidates. By doing this you will help to ensure that you have access to the best possible candidates for job positions. This approach was used by the corporate office of Eckerd Drug Company in St. Petersburg, Florida. Ed Nolan, the company's training director, provides this summary of their approach: "In the past, each of our six regions presented the results of their succession plan on a one-on-one basis to its vice president. The problem was that our regions were reluctant to release their hot, rising stars to other divisions. The solution that we've put into place is to recommend a joint review of the top two candidates from each region to all corporate officers."[12]

Strategies and Tactics for Excess Staff

Strategy 4: Find Alternative Uses for Staff

• **Search for temporary assignments.** Look for other departments that could use temporary assistance. Many companies have a variety of temporary cross-functional team assignments that last from six to eighteen months and that use volunteers from across the organization.

As a general guideline, look for projects that have high visibility, a targeted payoff, a definitive time frame, and leadership by one of your organization's senior managers. Whenever possible, avoid having your members become involved in standing committees.

• **Use available time to leapfrog anticipated projects.** If you know that a large-scale project will be assigned to your group during the next few months, use your additional staff to smooth the path for the project. This might involve:

- Meeting with other groups or organizations that have successfully managed similar projects to prepare for the types of problems your team may encounter as it moves through the project
- Having you or your members complete skill training required to support the project
- Performing any steps that can be taken far in advance of the project to facilitate its completion (e.g., procuring materials or laying out a project schedule)

• **Conduct a process review.** Most of the time people are too busy putting out fires to think about better methods of fire prevention. If you can't increase the quantity of your work, why not use this extra time to increase its quality? Select your team's most important work process and develop a plan for improving your performance on it.

• **Absorb additional functions.** Volunteer to assist other departments or divisions that lack the staff needed to perform some functions. If you find that other managers are hesitant to give up control, offer to share the responsibility for managing these functions. The strategy of managing team boundaries (discussed in Challenge 6) can help prevent misunderstandings or communication breakdowns on jointly managed functions.

Strategy 5: Present a Strong Defense

• **Determine the cost-effectiveness of going outside for help.** Do you know how much money it costs your company (salary, benefits, support staff, facilities, materials) to maintain your staff? What does it get for this investment, and how much would it cost to import comparable services from the outside? For example, if you manage recruiting, what is the cost of bringing a new hire on board? If you manage an information systems group, do you know how much it costs your department to develop new software programs, compared to the cost of purchasing them? Whenever possible, try to marshal figures to show that it would cost your organization more to purchase from outside agencies the services your team now provides.

• **Offer alternative cost reduction options.** When your team is about to be placed on the sacrificial altar of cost reduction, try offering alternative cost reduction proposals. For example, Terry Geraghty, director of organizational development for Harris Electronic Systems Sector, suggests, "If you are managing a recruiting function, translate the loss of recruiting dollars into the resulting loss of hirees. If your managers are pushing for a cost reduction, does it mean that you don't want to hire twenty people, or would it make more sense to maintain your recruiting level but limit it to candidates from your state to limit recruiting expenses?"[13]

• **Communicate the performance impact of staff losses.** If you are concerned that you may soon face a staff reduction, provide your managers with a written summary of those performance areas that are likely to be adversely affected by such a reduction. Focus on any disruptions to service or production that would:

- Be poorly received by your key internal and external customers
- Expose your organization to potential liability or safety problems
- Make it difficult for your organization to meet contractual or regulatory requirements

At the same time, alert your internal customers to potential service disruptions that might be created by staff reductions and see if they would be willing to argue your case on your behalf.

Strategy 6: Minimize the Impact of Staff Reductions

• **Use rotating layoffs as an option to downsizing.** Some organizations are opting to require employees to take off certain days without pay as an option to conducting a layoff. For example, this option is increasingly being used by school boards as an alternative to laying off teachers.

• **Transfer employees to contract status.** If worse comes to worst, this option enables you to reduce the overhead associated with medical and other benefits while allowing some employees to maintain some earning income. The tactic is being increasingly used to reduce the overhead costs associated with staff support functions, such as human resources, finance, and information systems. A strong cautionary note: before pursuing this option, you should review carefully IRS guidelines for determining the conditions that must be met before personnel can be classified as contract workers.

• **Provide part-time employment or job-sharing.** Find out whether it is possible to have employees convert from full-time to part-time status. Or see if different members are interested in taking part in a job-sharing arrangement in which they each cover the same job during different part-time shifts. Job sharing is particularly suited to groups such as customer service departments, whose members have a number of clearly defined and routine duties. It is less suitable for groups such as proposal teams, which deal with long-term projects requiring a high level of interdependent, coordinated action.

TOOL KIT

Team Transition Chart

The Team Transition Chart is designed to help you evaluate the degree to which your team has adequate coverage for its most important responsibilities, whether ongoing, routine activities or discrete projects.

I strongly recommend that you complete the chart as a team project. Create a rough sketch of the chart on a flipchart, then have members help you inventory your team's responsibilities and indicate their current level of involvement with each responsibility. If you are attempting to use the chart to provide more adequate coverage on work areas, invite members' suggestions on how best to do this. When reviewing the chart with your group, post the following questions:

- Where are we weak? Where do we lack adequate coverage?
- Do we lack balance? Is our workload fairly distributed?
- What priorities or time requirements are likely to change over the next year?
- Is there any confusion regarding each member's involvement in each activity?
- Are we spending an appropriate amount of time on high priority activities?

The model in Figure 5-1 shows a hypothetical transition chart for a training manager. Follow these steps to complete the chart (Figure 5-2):

1. *Responsibilities.* List your team's responsibilities in this column.
2. *Priority.* Determine the priority of each responsibility, using a scale of 1 to 5, with 5 representing critical priorities. Record these ratings in this column. If you have trouble doing this, you may find it useful to complete the Bull's-eye Exercise in this Tool Kit before going further.
3. *Customers.* Identify the key internal and external customers primarily served by each responsibility.
4. *Team Members.* Have the members of your group write their names or initials in these spaces.
5. For each responsibility, ask members to use the following legend to indicate their degree of involvement. They should record this information next to their name or initials.

    L   = Lead. Takes a lead role and has final say for this responsibility.

    I   = Involved. Involved in the responsibility but doesn't take a lead role in directing the responsibility.

    B   = Backup. Not currently assigned to this responsibility but is fully trained to perform as a backup.

    U   = Understands. Does not know how to perform the responsibility but understands its purpose, who is involved in it, and how it is applied by the team's customers. If the responsibility involves a discrete project, the member can answer questions pertaining to its current status.

    NA = Not Applicable. No knowledge of the responsibility.

6. *Time.* Have members calcuate the time (in number of hours) they usually invest in each responsibility each month, and re-

Figure 5-1. Example of the Team Transition Chart.

Responsibilities	Priority	Customers	Al	Ted	Mary	Don	TB	John	AP	JG	Total Time
Training:											
A. Teambuilding	5	Engineering	I/8	L/8	B		U			U	16
B. Quality Improvement	5	All Depts.		L/64	U		U				64
C. Needs Analysis Survey	4	All Depts.	U	U	U	L/7	U	I/3	U	U	10
D. Productive Leadership	3	All Depts.		L/16	U	I/16	I/8		I/8	U	48
E. Super Sales	4	Sales / Marketing	I/24		L/24	B	U			U	48
F. Effective Listening	2	All Depts.				B	U	I/16	I/8	U	24
Administrative:											
G. Negotiating Support	5	N/A								L/10	10
H. Budget Planning	5	N/A								L/16	16
I. Facilities Planning	4	N/A								L/24	24
Managing Vendors:											
J. Maintaining Files	1	N/A						I/8		L/8	16
K. Screening	2	N/A								L/16	16
L. New Course Develop.	4	N/A			I/10					L/30	40
M. Staff Evals.	5	N/A								L/16	16
		Total Times =	32	88	34	23	8	27	16	120	348

Team Members

L=Lead B=Backup I=Involved U=Understand NA=Not applicable

Figure 5-2. The Team Transition Chart.

Responsibilities	Priority	Customers	Team Members L=Lead B=Backup I=Involved U=Understand NA=Not applicable										Total Time
		Total Times =											

cord this information next to their name or initials. Total the hours for each responsibility under this column. These figures may have to be estimated for new work.

7. *Total Time.* Total the number of hours members have committed to these responsibilities to arrive at a total time commitment for your entire team.

The Team Transition Chart has several applications:

• *Time estimates.* The chart is an excellent tool for clearing up communication breakdowns and faulty assumptions. For example, you may find that no one has an accurate grasp of how much time is being spent on certain activities or that members provide widely varying estimates of the time that will be required to complete new projects.

• *Adequate coverage.* The chart provides a simple method for evaluating the degree to which each responsibility is adequately covered. For example, note that in the model Ted is the only person who is capable of directing the quality improvement training program. If Ted is terminated, transferred, or out sick, the team will not be able to provide this program. You can use the chart as a time-scheduling tool that can help you quickly determine the impact of events such as vacation schedules on key activities.

• *Skill development.* The chart enables you to determine the degree to which you are providing opportunities for cross-training members. Use the chart to determine whether members are being fully developed on the job and to plan assignments for new members.

• *Balanced delegation.* The chart can be used to determine whether workloads are being equitably balanced. It functions as an honesty index for determining the degree to which you are effectively delegating responsibilities and empowering employees. Note that in the model chart, the team's manager (JG) has absorbed complete control of routine administrative responsiblities, such as screening mail from potential vendors.

• *Role clarification.* Use the chart to prevent responsibilities that are jointly shared by several members from slipping between the cracks by clearly designating lead roles for each responsibility.

• *Staffing changes.* You can use the chart to determine the best method of shifting workloads to meet anticipated changes in responsibilities and staffing. For example, I know of several teams that used the Team Transition Chart to plan how best to close the gaps on work responsibilities after losing members through downsizings.

- *Efficiency.* Still another use of the chart is as a way to analyze your team's efficiency. Simply compare the hours that members spend on activities against estimated completion times for those activities.

- *Overall utilization.* By totaling your team's work hours you can determine its overall utilization level. Hours not listed on the chart usually involve small, nonvalue-added responsibilities such as running errands, engaging in phone conversations, and sorting mail. In addition, you can perform a quick comparison of assessed priority of responsibilities against the time spent on them. For example, note that in the model, although Maintaining Files is the training team's least important responsibility, sixteen hours each month are spent on this activity. What percentage of your team's available time is actually spent on significant responsibilities?

Team Benchmarking Chart

The Team Benchmarking Chart uses feedback from your manager, your internal customers, and benchmarked organizations to evaluate your group's readiness to assume new responsibilities and to determine how best to prepare your team to manage these responsibilities. Figure 5-3 shows how a hypothetical quality assurance team might prepare for the responsibility of introducing total quality management training to all employees. Follow these steps to complete the chart:

1. *Emerging Responsibilities.* After checking with your manager and finding out whether your internal customers will be asking you to support them with additional services, list all new responsibilities that your team will be taking over during the next few months. The Customer Interview Guidelines in Challenge 3 offer suggestions on how to uncover this information.
2. *Time frame.* Estimate the time period during which your team will initiate each new responsibility.
3. *Importance.* Rate the relative importance of each new responsibility on a scale of 1 to 5 , with 5 representing the most important.
4. *Skills.* Identify the most important technical skills needed to master each new responsibility. One of the best methods for obtaining this information is through the use of benchmarking with groups in other organizations that have successfully mastered these responsibilities.

Figure 5-3. Example of the Team Benchmarking Chart.

Emerging Responsibilities	Time Frame	I	Skills Required	L	Skills Acquisition
Total Quality Mgt. Training	12/94	5	• statistical process control • cause-and-effect analysis • process analysis	5 5 4	• N/A: in place • N/A: in place • conduct internally w/ materials from XYZ to reduce implementation costs
Direct, monitor, and coach cross-functional improvement teams:	2–5/95	5	• quality management cultures	2	• contact XYZ to deliver all training classes
• Train employees in team dynamics	3/95	3	• team facilitation	2	• have XYZ provide train-the-trainer
• Create the organization for teams (quality advisers, leaders, steering committee)	2/95	5	• knowledge of team dynamics	2	• use introductory program developed by corporate
• Track and monitor team performance	5/95	4	• set up quality data base • identify team performance measures	5 3	• N/A: in place • use model developed by sister division
• Facilitate initial teams	5/95	5	• team facilitation • coaching for assisting team leaders	2 2	• (same as above) • develop internally w/ input from sister division

5. *Competency Level.* Rate your team's current competency level, based on the following scale:

   5 = All members have mastered this skill area
   4 = Some members have mastered this skill area
   3 = Some members are moderately competent in this skill area
   2 = At least one member is moderately competent in this skill area
   1 = This is a completely new skill area for the team

6. *Skill Acquisition.* Describe all possible options for increasing your team's strength in this skill area and for importing the skill from outside sources. Again, use benchmarking to assess accurately the relative advantages of attempting to graft these skills on to your team compared to purchasing them from the outside.

When reviewing this chart with your team, try to address the following questions:

- What is the most important gap between our current team strength and our emerging responsibilities?
- What is the likely impact of not developing this skill area?
- What is the most reasonable option for acquiring the skill? Is it worth the effort required to develop an in-house capability in this skill area? Do we have the time needed to do this? Would it be more effective to import the skill from the outside?
- What is the earliest point at which we will need to use this skill?

Bull's-Eye Exercise

This simple exercise can help your team leverage its performance by distinguishing between critical and noncritical activities and identifying activities that can be easily eliminated or transferred to other groups. Follow these steps to complete this exercise with your team:

1. Begin by drawing on a flipchart a bull's-eye similar to that in Figure 5-4.
2. In the center of the bull's-eye briefly describe the core mission of your team—how you view the value added by your team to your organization. As team missions frequently change in response to larger organizational changes, you may need to give some serious thought to this mission description.

Figure 5-4.   The Bull's-Eye Chart.

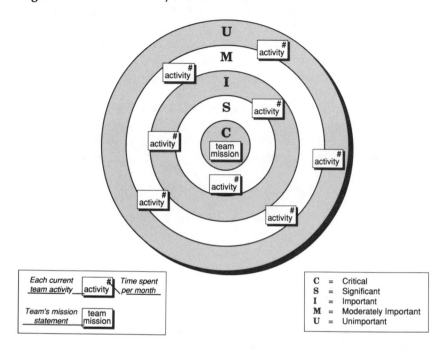

3. Next, ask members to help you list on cards all the work activities currently performed by your team.
4. In the upper right corner of each card, ask members to estimate the amount of time the team spends on the activity each month.
5. After you've completed this list, tape each card to the appropriate area of the bull's-eye, using the following legend:

   C = Activities *critical* to the success of your mission
   S = Activities *significant* to the success of your mission
   I = Activities *important* to the success of your mission
   M = Activities *moderately important* to the success of your mission
   U = Activities *unimportant* to the success of your mission

6. Set a goal for the amount of time you would like to save by off-loading moderately important or unimportant activities to other groups.
7. Once all cards have been placed on the flipchart, determine if any cards listed in the U space could be given to another team.

8. Total the estimated time that could be saved by eliminating or transferring these activities. If you still haven't met your goal, proceed to the M area to eliminate any activities.
9. After selecting activities for transfer, work with your team to identify the groups that would be most appropriate for absorbing these activities. Remember to consider not only groups within your department but other departments, divisions, and perhaps even your corporate office.
10. Consider the most effective method of approaching these other groups and your manager to explore together the possibility of shifting these activities.

If you don't feel that you have the time to conduct this exercise with your team, post the Bull's-eye Chart for a week, provide members with note cards, and invite them to add cards throughout the week as they think of entries. Then perform a joint review of the Bull's-eye over a working lunch.

The Bull's-eye Exercise has several applications.

1. *As a developmental exercise.* By performing this exercise as a team, you can provide members with a better overall picture of your team's activities and focus. This is especially valuable when you've recently brought new members on board or when members are frequently isolated by shift, location, or time pressure.

2. *As a tool for reassessing your organizational mission.* Because this exercise begins with a review of your team's core mission, it forces everyone to take a fresh look at your team's mission statement. If you are spending a disproportionate amount of time on activities that are unrelated to your core mission, it's either because (1) you've allowed yourself to be sidetracked by unimportant activities, or (2) your core mission has gradually shifted over time.

A good example of the second situation occurred in a sales team for a major manufacturer of long-distance electronic communication systems. This team had been involved primarily in the sales of isolated hardware components in the domestic market. After completing the exercise, the team discovered that its activities increasingly were centering around the delivery of field support services, such as facilities planning and technical training, for communication systems being installed in remote locations. Eventually, as the result of a series of discussions that began with this exercise, the team decided to revise its mission statement to reflect the changing role it was being asked to play in the organization.

3. *As a vehicle for negotiating priorities and time schedules.* You can use the chart as a starting point for discussions with your manager regarding priorities and scheduling. Your manager can help you make certain that your team is focused on activities that are firmly linked to executive-level objectives. In addition, your manager may provide information that could lead you to revise the priorities that you've assigned to various activities. On the other hand, managers sometimes hand off activities without first carefully assessing the impact that the changes will have on a group's overall schedule. If you've encountered this problem, you can use the chart to help your manager better understand the time trade-offs involved in working on certain activities at the expense of others.

4. *As a first step in evaluating team responsibilities.* You can use the Bull's-eye Chart as the first stage in completing the Team Transition Chart in the Tool Kit. To do this, simply convert your ratings to the following numbers and place them in the Ratings column of the Team Transition Chart: C = 5, S = 4, I = 3, M = 2, and U = 1.

Supplemental Staff Questionnaire

Use the following questions to help plan the most effective way to manage volunteers, student interns, and loaned employees from other departments:

1. *Do you have a clear idea of the duties you wish to assign to these individuals?* Before bringing anyone else on board, evaluate your activities and identify those activities that don't require a lot of supervision and in which other people could be easily trained.

2. *Are you expecting volunteers or interns to perform grunt work, such as stuffing envelopes, or will you be providing them with opportunities to use their skills?* Many nonprofit organizations, such as the Red Cross, that rely on large numbers of volunteers are increasingly finding that many of its volunteers are coming from professional backgrounds and are reluctant to work as simply another set of helping hands.[14] Instead, these organizations look for ways to apply the volunteers' professional skills to their assignments. Are you sure that you will be making full use of the skills and abilities of the people you will be bringing on board?

3. *How do you plan to clarify your expectations and the types of training and support that you will be able to provide these individuals?* Make certain

that you clearly define the commitments these individuals will be asked to take on and the length of time they will be expected to work with your team. Many volunteers like to know that they are being asked to provide support for a clearly defined, short-term period. College students must juggle their schedules to accommodate internships and need to know the hours they will be expected to be working onsite. Remember that volunteers and interns will require some training and instruction in advance of their assignments. Make certain that you will obtain a favorable return on the time investment you will be making. Clarify up-front any support you will provide regarding travel expenses, meals, or salary (if applicable). Some organizations, such as the Red Cross, routinely provide volunteers with job descriptions to prevent mismatching between volunteers and job assignments. Others, such as the Girl Scouts, make use of volunteer agreements to formalize the commitment in time and responsibilities that volunteers are being asked to take on.[15]

4. *Have you clearly defined reporting relationships between you and your volunteers?* If you are borrowing employees from other departments, clarify the reporting relationships that they will have with you and their full-time managers during the time they are assigned to you. For example, who will be making their scheduling decisions and handling their routine personnel matters? If they will be working for you for several weeks or months, will you be asked to provide input for their yearly appraisals?

5. *Have you provided these individuals with clear, targeted assignments?* Whenever possible, have them focus their efforts on a single major project instead of a variety of small, discrete activities. This will reduce your training requirement and make it easier for them to self-manage their work. In addition, at the conclusion of their volunteer period, they will have a greater sense of achievement.

6. *How do you plan to provide feedback and recognition?* Build a solid feedback and recognition process into your efforts. Provide volunteers with plaques and take them out to lunch with your team at the conclusion of their assignment. Provide student interns with formal evaluations and recommendations that may be helpful to them in securing employment. If you are borrowing employees from other departments, send their manager a nice letter acknowledging the fine work that they have done for you. Actions such as this will increase the likelihood that you will get additional volunteers.

Notes

1. Interview with Terry Geraghty, director of organizational development for Harris Electronic Systems Sector, March 1993.
2. Dave Aiielinski, "Cutting Cycle Times Is Essential for Meeting Customer Demands," *Total Quality Newsletter* (January 1991), pp. 1–4.
3. Interview with Brian Chitester, director of process improvement for Pepsi Cola, June 1993.
4. William J. Doerr, "Manage Time, Double Sales," *Managers Magazine* (May 1989), pp. 4–12.
5. Interview with Jane Rose, training manager for the city of Lakeland, Florida, May 1993.
6. Interview with Mark Johnson, manager of quality curriculum for AT&T Paradyne, April 1993.
7. Interview with Terry Geraghty.
8. Sara P. Noble, ed., *301 Great Management Ideas from America's Most Innovative Small Companies* (Boston: Goldhirsh Group, 1991), p. 224. Printed with permission, *Inc.* magazine, 1991. © 1991 by Goldhirsh Group, Inc., 38 Commercial Wharf, Boston, MA 02110.
9. Noble, *301 Great Management Ideas*, p. 108.
10. Interview with Jane Rose.
11. Interview with Bob Stephens, human resources supervisor for 3M Springfield plant, June 1993.
12. Interview with Ed Nolan, training director for Eckerd Drug Company, May 1993.
13. Interview with Terry Geraghty.
14. Beverly Gerber, "Managing Volunteers," *Training* (June 1991), pp. 21–26.
15. Ibid.

Challenge 6

Forge Alliances

Politics as a Social Reality

How would you describe someone who has gained a reputation in his company as being a master of organizational politics? When I ask this question in my management workshops, I typically hear the following kinds of adjectives: *self-serving, phony, superficial, dishonest, manipulative,* or *evasive.*

In other words, political competence conveys a negative connotation. I'd like to offer an alternative view—that the art of organizational politics is an essential managerial survival skill. To appreciate better the importance of political skills, think of your organization as an automobile engine. No matter how well an engine is designed and manufactured or how fine the tolerances between engine parts, it needs a proper lubricant to run smoothly. Otherwise the engine will quickly freeze up as increasing heat causes the pistons to lock into the engine cylinders. Because it's impossible to achieve a perfect alignment between engine parts, we depend upon oil to provide the amount of "give" necessary to enable engine parts to mesh together correctly. In the same way, because an organization is not an ideal system it depends upon managers who understand, and can succeed within, the political realities of the workplace.

The need for political competence is especially important in today's turbulent and high-pressure workplace. Within the average work environment, we typically find that the following five factors generate additional friction between groups.

1. *Us vs. Them.* When people fear that even small performance problems will lead to the loss of their jobs, finger pointing and ducking for cover become the norm, and increased adversarial relationships develop between departments and groups. We tend to view those individuals with whom we most interact—our internal customers, suppli-

ers, and support groups—as the cause of our problems, rather than focusing our attention on those large-scale events that actually drive the change process. An example to illustrate this group polarization process was related by Bank of America's vice president Robert Beck. In an interview for the *HRMagazine*, Robert explained that teamwork among his company's groups was severely challenged during the years 1985–1988, when his organization experienced a significant restructuring and downsizing: "There's a natural tendency for the wagons to circle whenever there is a serious threat. We had to make sure that there was one big circle. The worst scenario is to have a lot of small circles shooting at each other. Infighting can be extremely unproductive, with people getting hit in the cross fire."[1]

2. *The Walled Fortress.* During tough times, managers try to protect themselves by insulating themselves from other groups. Like medieval lords confronting a plague, they pull up the drawbridges around their little fortresses and hide behind their walls, hoping that the plague (downsizing, reorganization, increasing work pressure) will soon pass.

Both the greatest strength and the greatest weakness of a fortress is its impermeability; nothing gets in or out. In the same way, when we wall ourselves in to protect ourselves from hostile forces, we also cut ourselves off from the information, resources, and critical feedback that is essential for any team's survival.

3. *The Limited Pie.* Another contributing factor is the "limited pie" fallacy, which is based on the false assumption that the more one person gets, the less is available for someone else. When people buy into this belief, information and resources tend to be hoarded in the hope that control of these factors will provide a small margin of job security. In addition to creating bottlenecks and work slowdowns, this problem generates excessive waste. I know of one company in which the failure to consolidate material and part shipments resulted in a high level of waste in materials procurement. As another example, I was asked by three different managers in one organization to provide their separate groups with similar training services. None of these department managers took the initiative to explore the option of placing all the projects under the same contract (which would have resulted in less paperwork and expense for them). Some time later I found that another department had contracted with one of our competitors to provide the same type of service! In this company, time and money were wasted because each manager focused only on his or her own needs.

4. *Organizational Pressure.* As we discussed in Challenge 2, organizations that are going through accelerated change tend to be high-

stress environments. When employees are overwhelmed and grossly fatigued, they may feel that it takes all their energy simply to get through the work day. Stressed-out employees are more prone to conflicts and turf battles as everyone frantically maneuvers to place himself in the most advantageous position (usually at the cost of good work relationships). The result is that if your group is experiencing a high degree of stress, you will need to work even harder to maintain good communication with other groups.

5. *Shifting Relationships and Alliances.* While it's easy to assume that internal alliances are self-perpetuating, nothing is further from the truth. If your organization is undergoing rapid change, frequently the first thing that will give way will be those support networks that you've painstakingly established throughout your company. Mentors are reassigned, managers with whom you've developed solid working relationships are terminated, and groups are consolidated. The point is that no matter how successful you've been in the past in forging alliances, you can't sit on your laurels and take your internal relationships for granted. To survive in this kind of environment you need to work continuously at building new relationships and strengthening existing ones.

These five factors suggest that political skills become more important during times of rapid organizational change. Without managers who can apply political savvy, many organizations would soon freeze up and come to a standstill.

Importance of Allies

The art of office politics is essentially the art of knowing how to forge alliances with other managers and groups. During tough times, organizational allies can provide you with several benefits:

1. Having allies means that you don't have to go it alone. Allies can help you obtain needed resources, secure your job, and may even (at some point in the future) be in a position to hire you. Even if they lack such power, allies are often able to connect you to those people who can help you.

2. Allies can provide you with the support you need to accomplish your objectives. Moreover, they serve as a strong line of defense if you find yourself unfairly maligned or attacked by others in your organization.

3. In line with the strategies and tactics discussed in Challenge 1, allies are an important part of your early-warning systems. They help you remain well embedded in the organizational informational network and can keep you alerted to a variety of impending dangers or opportunities, ranging from reorganizations to job openings.

4. Allies increase your perceived credibility and usefulness in the eyes of others by providing you with opportunities to demonstrate your skills and accomplishments and by conveying to others the value you add to your company. In addition, allies extend your range of influence within your organization.

5. Allies can provide an important support buffer for warding off needless stress and frustration.

6. Allies serve as an essential honesty index for checking out approaches to problems and helping you troubleshoot decisions.

7. Finally, and perhaps most important, if you can convert potential enemies to allies you don't have to divert critical time and energy from key organizational goals to the nonproductive and mutually destructive pastimes of infighting, backstabbing, and safeguarding.

Principles behind Positive Politics

Although I've suggested that the mastery of office politics is a key survival skill, this doesn't mean that all political approaches are the same. Just as dirty oil can "gunk up" an engine, so too can negative politics place additional stress and strain on the workplace. What separates individuals who practice negative politics from those who practice positive politics is that the latter adhere to the following seven basic principles in all their political interactions.

1. *They view others as potential partners.* Positive political players operate on the assumption that everyone in the organization is a potential partner. They assume that people who try to undermine their efforts are not opponents but merely partners who have temporarily lost the larger view of the organization's overall goals. They continually strive to help others retain this big-picture focus.

2. *They try to understand their partners' views.* This principle ties directly into one of Stephen Covey's seven success principles, which is "seek first to understand, then to be understood."[2] Positive political players take the time to understand the workings of their partners' processes and how their partners are affected by their actions and deci-

sions. (Challenge 3 contains several tools designed to help you see through the eyes of your customers.)

3. *They respect their partners' concerns.* They understand that during tough times it's sometimes difficult for other people to lower their defenses and overcome feelings of fear and distrust. They try to anticipate their partners' concerns and are careful not to discount or belittle these concerns, no matter how unsupported the concerns may be by their own experiences. They know that a starting point for dialogue involves appreciating the risk their partners' take in moving away from managerial game playing to open dialogue.

4. *They are honest in their dealings with their partners.* When dealing with others, positive political players strive to be tactful and sensitive without sacrificing honesty. If they have an objection with an issue, they lay it on the table for discussion. If they are having difficulty working with a person, their first course of action is to try to work out the problem directly with that individual, rather than relying on manipulation or outside coercion.

5. *They make and keep commitments.* Honesty is closely tied with making and keeping commitments. If they say something, they mean it. If they indicate that they will take action on a problem, they do so. They manage their personal and professional relationships with a high level of integrity. They don't set one deadline on the table and keep another one in their pocket. If they can't keep a commitment, they accept responsibility for their failure and alert their partners to it as quickly as possible.

6. *Whenever possible, they deal directly and informally.* Positive political players don't hide behind memoranda. They aren't afraid to deal directly with people. As an example, some time ago, I was called in to provide team building to a group that was suffering from a number of performance problems, including bottlenecks in its work processes. I quickly found out that two of the team's managers, who were located at a remote site not more than ten feet apart from each other in the same double-width trailer, were sending each other daily memos (with copies to their mutual boss, to protect their own flanks), rather than discussing their problems face to face! Small wonder that this team was having difficulty moving forward.

7. *They remain flexible.* Positive political players don't regard their policies as sacred writings or their work procedures as concrete fixtures. They recognize the need to continually adapt their own approaches to keep pace with changes in their organization. In addition, they are personally flexible. They periodically perform self-audits to

examine the effectiveness of their interpersonal skills and the strength of their work relationships.

Warning Symptoms

The following warning signs may indicate that organizational isolation is likely to become a critical management issue for your team:

❑ Relationships are rapidly deteriorating between your team and other groups or departments.

❑ There is a lot of finger pointing. People spend more time on self-protective activities than on getting the job done.

❑ Other departments have withdrawn their support. You feel that if you were suddenly to encounter a serious work problem, no one would come to your rescue.

❑ Decision-making sessions with other groups and departments quickly turn into win-lose battles.

❑ You feel that your team is increasingly cut off from information, resources, and influence in your organization.

Strategies

The Alliance Pyramid (Figure 6-1) illustrates the interrelationship among the three success strategies introduced in this chapter.

Figure 6-1. The Alliance Pyramid.

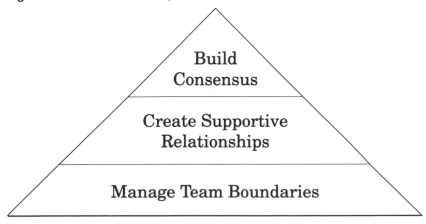

The foundation strategy is to manage team boundaries. To predict the occurrence of earthquakes, seismologists carefully map the location of major fault lines—areas in which the large plates that make up the earth's crust rub up against each other, producing great stress and, through occasional realignment, earthquakes. In the same way, the strategy of boundary management involves exploring the organizational fault lines, that is, the lines of interface between your team and other teams. These fault lines are continually shifting because of changes in your organization, your team's mission, and the relationships that bind your team to other groups. To master this strategy you need to be able to understand these changes and make them work to your advantage. This strategy has been placed at the base of the pyramid because it involves your team's position within your entire organization and because it serves as an essential foundation for the development of the other two strategies.

Another component of this strategy involves repositioning your team to assume a stronger, more central role in your organization. The tactic of repositioning is based on the premise that your ability to forge alliances and influence others is largely a function of how other groups view your team's organizational role. While it's true that a team's role is partially defined by its charter and job description, I often find that managers underestimate the degree of mobility they have in repositioning their teams within their organizations.

The second strategy is to create supportive relationships. This strategy has been placed in the middle of the Alliance Pyramid to indicate that, in contrast to the broader strategy of managing team processes and functions, it deals with the more targeted area of building strong relationships with other key managers.

When organizations move through difficult times, there is always the prevalent fear among managers that negotiations with other groups must take the form of a no-holds-barred, winner-take-all struggle. These types of win-lose conflicts become battles of attrition that eventually wear down both winners and losers. The strategy of managing relationships can help protect you from becoming a victim of this kind of organizational cannibalism, which thrives within tough business environments. In this strategy, we focus on how to build a network of supportive relationships through such tactics as creating partnerships in your work, strengthening interteam communication links, trading hostages, selecting a level playing field, and separating yourself from the target.

The third strategy is to build consensus with other managers on work issues. This strategy has been placed at the pinnacle of the pyramid to show that it is the most targeted of the three strategies, focusing as it does on the day-to-day communication skills necessary for the care and feeding of good work relationships. The strategy of building consensus involves having a clear focus on your aims and objectives when dealing with other groups, understanding their expectations and concerns, knowing how to uncover and overcome areas of resistance, and being able to seek alignment on issues.

Strategy 1: Manage Team Boundaries

- **Analyze your relationships with other groups.** Before starting out on a journey, it's nice to know where you are currently located in relationship to your destination. When your goal is to forge organizational alliances, knowing your current position means having a clear picture of how your team interacts with other interdependent groups. There are several methods for analyzing team relationships, including Relationship Maps, team assessment surveys, interviews and focus groups, and Performance Maps.

1. *Relationship Maps.* A Relationship Map (Figure 6-2) provides a simple picture of how your team interacts with other groups. It usually includes such elements as:

- Areas of interdependency between yourself and other organizational groups
- Critical fault lines—the processes and functions that generate the greatest stress in your relationships with other groups and that represent the greatest potential for interteam conflicts
- Anticipated operational changes that could significantly affect your team's working relationships with other groups, such as changes in organizational mission, operational policies and procedures, the capabilities of suppliers and support groups, changing customer requirements, or your team's resources and bench strength

A Relationship Map provides a variety of useful information. It offers an overview of what might otherwise be a confusing maze of relationships. It can be used to quickly identify potential trouble spots in your team's relationships with other groups. By creating the map as a team project, your members can also obtain a better appreciation of how team relationships affect their performance. In addition, you will frequently find that members will be able to add additional detail to your map. For example, a member who has been working closely with one of your customers may recommend that you include on the map

Figure 6-2.   The Relationship Map.

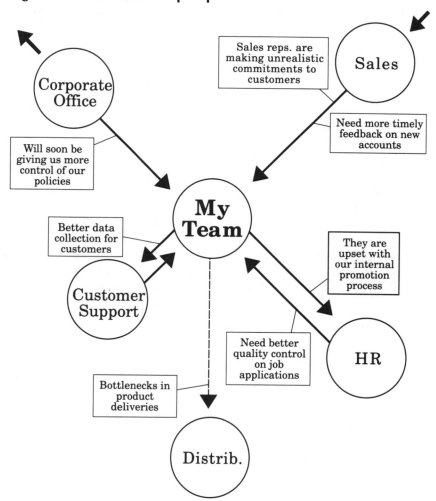

needs or requirements that haven't as yet been expressed formally by your customers. Another member may be able to offer suggestions for easing the tension along certain organizational fault lines.

The Tool Kit for this challenge contains instructions for creating a Relationship Map, an example of a map, and guidelines for using your completed map to forge stronger relationships with other groups.

2. *Team Assessment Surveys.* Another way to determine how well your team is performing with other groups is to make use of one of the many team assessment surveys that are commercially available.

Before using a team assessment survey, you should consider the following cautions:

- There is a critical difference between surveys designed to analyze the performance of individual teams and those designed to evaluate relationshps among two or more teams. The former focus primarily on evaluating intrateam relationships and roles, whereas the latter focus on analyzing processes and functions that flow across teams.
- A well-designed survey process should include input from both team managers and a good representation of all members. It's a good idea to get the other manager(s) involved at an early stage in the selection of the survey instrument you will use. Also, before using the survey, reach agreement with the other participating managers regarding the anonymity of survey feedback, who will compile the data, who will have access to survey reports, and how survey reports will be used.
- Because you want to make certain that both teams are assured that survey results are impartially prepared, you should seriously consider having an impartial third party (someone with experience in survey analysis) compile the data and develop a summary report on this data.
- Always choose a survey that is easily understandable and interpretable by you and the other survey participants. Stay away from surveys that use psychobabble. The items in a well-designed team assessment survey should be clearly related to the work issues that you would like to review with the other teams.

3. *Interviews and Focus Groups.* Another way of determining how effectively your group is interacting with other groups is through the use of individual interviews and focus groups—sessions in which small groups of individuals are asked to provide feedback on a series of pretargeted work issues. Both of these techniques require the use of an organizational development specialist. Although interviews and focus group sessions provide more detailed data than surveys, they require more time and (if run by outside consulting firms) can be more expensive.

Before initiating this step, meet with your team to identify the types of questions that you would like to see covered in the interviews or focus groups; then ask the other manager do the same with his or her team. Finally, review each other's list and make certain that all questions are specifically targeted and that none are worded in such a way as to imply criticisms of each others' teams.

4. *Performance Maps.* The Performance Map, which was introduced in Challenge 3, can help you identify areas in which your team is having difficulty meeting the needs of your customers. This tool also has the reverse application; it can be used to help your internal suppliers explore ways to support your team better. Examples of how the Performance Map can be applied and instructions for its use are presented in the Tool Kit for Challenge 3.

• **Take steps to manage team boundaries.** This tactic involves working with other managers to improve the performance of processes or functions that flow across the boundaries of your respective teams. This could involve situations in which:

- One team functions as a supplier to the other
- One team is in a supporting role to the other
- Both teams have joint responsibility for managing certain key functions or for making decisions that affect each other's operation

Let's take a look at three techniques for managing team boundaries, suggestions for applying each technique, cautions related to their use, and tools for facilitating their implementation.

Technique 1: Contracting—The creation of explicit written agreements that teams agree to follow when providing one another with services, meeting each other's requirements, or co-managing functions.

Applications:

- Especially applicable when the same procedures or methods are not consistently followed by all members of each team
- Useful for resolving team turf battles over the ownership of functions

Cautions:

- Involves a high level of risk taking and diplomacy
- May require the use of a trained facilitator
- Managers must have the authority to commit their teams to agreements
- Contracts should be periodically reviewed and updated to meet changing conditions

Tools:

- The Team Contracting Chart (in the Tool Kit) can be used to help you work through contracting discussions with other managers.
- If-Then Decision Chart (in the Tool Kit) is designed for situa-

tions in which team management issues involve a number of interacting variables.

Technique 2: Process Analysis—a flowchart showing the sequential steps involved in a process and analysis of ways to improve performance on selected process steps.

Applications:

- Useful for resolving team conflicts concerning processes or for working with other groups to design new processes
- Helps avoid finger pointing on problems and to position team conflicts as improvement opportunities
- Helps to strengthen your team's performance by providing members with a more solid understanding of processes

Cautions:

- All process stakeholders (groups affected by the process) need to have input in this effort
- If performed correctly, it can require a heavy time investment
- Requires all stakeholders to reach agreement on process measures and accurate data collection and to be willing to examine processes with open minds

Technique 3: Interteam Ground Rules—establishing with other groups a written code of conduct that the members of your respective teams agree to follow when interacting with each other.

Applications:

- Useful when conflicts with other teams are created by communication breakdowns or poor communication between groups
- Useful whenever members are spread out and required to take independent action in representing your team

Cautions:

- The guidelines you select should be behavioral and observable. For example, saying, "Each team will agree to get back to the other on phone requests or questions within four hours of the initial call" is better than "Each team will try to be more responsive to each other."
- Teams tend to approach this technique with a certain amount of defensiveness. Invite the other manager to share his or her suggestions before offering your own ideas.
- It's important to get across to all participants that these guidelines are not policing actions for your respective teams, nor do

they represent an implied criticism of past performance. They simply make explicit the types of professional behavior which supports positive team relationships.

Tools:

- None provided

- **Strengthen your team's organizational image.** You can look for ways to improve your team's performance and the professional image members present to other groups. If you feel that this point is a minor one, think back to the last time you called another department inside your company, and your call was answered by someone who came across as being rude or disinterested. Or consider the poor image departments project when they fail to follow up on requests for information or assistance.

Like it or not, each team member represents your entire team to others, and your job success is largely dependent upon the type of professional image that your team presents to your company and to outside organizations. Team image management becomes even more important when your company is going through tough times and is critically evaluating the contribution potential of each group.

The Team Boundary Planning Chart in the Tool Kit is helpful when you are trying to encourage the members of your team to reach agreement regarding the guidelines they will follow when representing your team to other groups.

Strategy 2: Create Supportive Relationships

- **Make your colleagues your partners.** This tactic involves building relationships by exploring ways you and other managers can provide each other with support, assistance, and feedback on team performance.

1. *Understand each other's work processes.* As a starting point, consider asking other managers to provide your team with brief training or coaching sessions on processes that directly affect your group. A finance manager can provide information on the budget reporting process; a purchasing manager can report on the correct way to expedite emergency orders. These types of learning experiences can help your team develop a better appreciation of how other groups perform and the challenges they are facing. Another important payoff is that this approach can help your team effectively manage key processes, resulting in reduced waste and lost time. Still another benefit is that this training process serves as an opportunity to build face-to-face part-

nerships between the members of your respective teams. The flip side of this learning approach is to offer other managers the opportunity to train their groups on your team's processes. A version of this training involves working out an arrangement in which you and other managers agree to provide each other with information briefings on changes in methods, procedures, or policies that affect both teams.

Another method you can use to learn about other processes or to encourage other groups to provide feedback on your processes is the *process walk-through,* one of the key elements of process analysis. In this technique, members physically walk through the steps of a process and interview the indiviuals who conduct those steps to look for areas for improvement. In a similar fashion, you could invite other managers to accompany your team as it completes important tasks to enable the managers to get a better feel for how their actions affect your team.

Not long ago I conducted a team-building workshop with two teams, both of which were involved in the management of public lands. One group (the internal supplier) was responsible for the purchase of tracts of land; the other group (its customer) was responsible for managing the land. For some time, the second group had been trying to alert the first group to a critical problem: The first group was purchasing land tracts without simultaneously purchasing access rights to those tracts from the owners of the adjacent properties. (Access rights enable the agency to cross private property to get to publicly owned landsites.) The breakthrough came when the supplier was invited to accompany the customer to visit a newly purchased land parcel and see for himself the difficulties that were created by this situation.

Some U.S. companies have recently begun to import a Japanese version of the process walk-through, known as the *kokai* watch, in which a group is observed by a team made up of individuals from other company groups as it performs an activity. In another version of the *kokai* watch, a team takes apart products to look for defects or to examine the product from the viewpoint of someone who is required to operate or service it. *Kokai* watches have been found to produce excellent improvements in such areas as machine serviceability, changeover time, increased efficiency, and the spotting of potential safety hazards. An excellent example of how a *kokai* watch operates is presented in Mary Walton's book, *Deming Management at Work* (Putnam's, 1990).

The premise behind the process walk-through and the *kokai* watch is that sometimes a fresh pair of eyes, somewhat detached from a work process or product, can provide valuable insights into ways to improve those processes and products. A strong secondary benefit is that these techniques help groups build partnerships by providing them with a common language and knowledge base.

Before undertaking either of these techniques, it is necessary to build a high trust level with those individuals whose processes will be under observation. Otherwise, these individuals may view these techniques as fault-finding mechanisms and may hide performance problems or be reluctant to disclose information about their processes.

2. *Provide each other with performance feedback.* Another way to create partnerships is to look for ways that you and other groups can provide each other with useful feedback about your teams. One way to do this is through the use of the Performance Map and the Customer Interview Guidelines, both of which are included in the Tool Kit for Challenge 3. These techniques are particularly well suited for situations in which you want to obtain information from internal or external customers or provide performance feedback to your suppliers.

If you want to communicate to your customers that you are trying to make your team more responsive to their requirements, consider inviting them to provide you with feedback that you can fold into your team's annual performance appraisals or your developmental planning sessions.

3. *Seek input on key decisions.* One of the quickest ways to overcome resistance is to ask other departments to be stakeholders in your decision process. An example of how this works was provided by Jim Yager, assistant executive director of management services for the South Florida Water Management District: "Our Information Systems department made a lot of decisions that impacted a lot of people and didn't keep other departments properly informed of these decisions. Now, we bring back all major decisions to the Technology Management Advisory Committee, made up of myself and my stakeholders. We test alternatives, jointly analyze the pros and cons of different options."[3]

According to Jim, these changes have greatly strengthened the performance of his company's IS department and enhanced teamwork between this department and other groups.

4. *Use a buddy system.* Buddy systems are agreements made between managers about ways they can support each other as advisers or troubleshooters. These agreements can be arrived at on a one-on-one basis by yourself and another manager, or they can encompass a larger group of managers.

A good illustration of how buddy systems can be used was provided by Ed Nolan, vice president of human resources for Eckerd Drug Company:

> We have six regional field offices which normally oper-
> ate independently of each other, with little cross-fertiliza-
> tion of ideas. Last week we had two adjoining regions in
> our Loss Prevention group get together, and I presented a
> session on creative thinking so that we could break the mold
> and encourage them to think about doing their business in
> a different fashion and to share ideas.
>
> Workshop participants are now going to do this [net-
> working] on an extended basis with adjacent regions
> throughout the company. One of the assignments that
> members had coming out of this workshop was to pick a
> partner from the other region and to call that person twice
> a month. The other person can serve as a troubleshooter,
> devil's advocate, and sounding board for problem solving.
> In addition, because these people are in our Loss Prevention
> department, when they need a partner to conduct a particu-
> larly sensitive investigation, such as a sexual harassment
> charge, or a pharmacist who is suspected of diverting
> drugs—the types of things that put you under tremendous
> risk if you make an accusation—they are now empowered
> to call someone from another region to come in as a partner.
> Such a partner conducts a coinvestigation and can bring in
> an objective point of view.[4]

• **Strengthen interteam communications.** The second tactic for building better relationships with other managers is to strengthen teamwork between your respective teams and to ensure that informa-tion on changes and decisions can be quickly passed through your teams.

1. *Use bonding experiences.* Bonding experiences bring teams to-gether in a relaxed and comfortable manner. One way to do this is through the many ropes-and-pulleys courses marketed by team-build-ing consultants. The courses require the members of different teams, or all members of a single team, to work together to overcome a variety of physical challenges. Another technique is to place different groups in a friendly competitive situation. For example, one of our clients sponsors an annual three-day contest each year during work hours that includes events such as a tug-of-war contest in a muddy area and a miniature tricycle race. Watching a high-powered executive zipping

through an obstacle course on a tricycle tends to make that person seem a little less intimidating and a little more approachable. Each group sponsors its own team for the race and wears the same colored tee-shirts. There is an entry fee for each event, and all proceeds go to the local Special Olympics organization.

If riding tricycles isn't your style, you could approach other managers with the idea of having selected members from your respective teams sent off together to the same seminars or training workshops. Other options include having members from different groups jointly conduct benchmarking visits to other organizations or visits to customers' sites. These types of experiences provide groups with opportunities to build strong personal relationships that carry back to the job.

2. *Expedite day-to-day communications.* Sometimes relationships with other groups suffer because the groups are separated by location, schedule, or work pressure. In such cases, communications between groups tend to be strained and rushed. Consider the possibility of having the members of your respective groups meet for an hour to brainstorm ways to increase the effectiveness of your day-to-day communications. Some of the options that you might consider are:

- Making use of electronic mail systems
- Conducting brown-bag discussions or lunch-and-learns with the other team
- Making a list of the types of information to which you have access (minutes of meetings, status reports, consultant evaluations, project schedules) that would be very useful to other groups, and compiling a second list that includes the types of information that you would like to receive from the other groups
- Occasionally inviting representatives of other groups to sit in on your team meetings when discussing projects that will affect the operation of those groups
- Placing a process flowchart diagram on a wall near a common work area (if your respective teams are jointly involved in a process improvement project and you are located near each other) and inviting members from both teams to place sticky notes next to selected process steps to diagram their ideas regarding observed performance problems or suggestions for improving these problems

- **Trading hostages.** The third tactic involves building relationships by providing members or different teams with opportunities to work within each other's team. This can be achieved through job rotation or by having members of other groups take on developmental assignments within your team (Strategies 3 and 4 in Challenge 5 provide examples of this). Another method involves placing members of different teams in the same work area.

Two excellent examples of trading hostages are provided by Joe Dunsmore, senior marketing manager for AT&T Paradyne:

> At Paradyne we have a huge time/distance problem and language problem between us and our Japan subsidiary. To help overcome these problems we've established a job rotation program to establish empathy between these two business units. Someone from our Japanese office spends a year in Florida to serve in a support function for Japan—sort of a regional champion for Japan. One of the things that the company and the individual get out of it is that the individual carries back to Japan a much better understanding of corporate's requirements and the requirements that corporate must place on AT&T Paradyne/Japan as a supplier. Another benefit is that the loaned professional builds much stronger English skills.
>
> Another example is how we resolved a communication problem between our engineering group in New Jersey and a group in Florida. We determined that we needed to physically move some of engineering team members to Florida and others to New Jersey to ensure close teaming on critical R&D projects. Sharing a location with product management and marketing team members became a secondary benefit."[5]

• **Separate yourself from the target.** As you attempt to build strong interteam relationships, you may occasionally inherit problems from your predecessors (if you are new to the position) or from your manager. Or you may be the bearer of bad news, such as an order to implement an unpopular program (downsizing is a good example) that has been mandated by your executive management or corporate office.

Faced with any of these situations, your challenge is to separate yourself from the target. This means keeping the anger and frustration that other managers are experiencing from overflowing into your relationships with them. The following guidelines can help you separate yourself from the target:

1. *Serve as translator.* Sometimes the anger and frustration you encounter result from the fact that a good action or decision has been

poorly communicated through the organization. Before responding to others' complaints, draw them out concerning what they know of the situation and correct any misunderstandings that they might have.

2. *Give other managers a chance to ventilate.* This holds true regardless of whether you are taking over for another manager, have found yourself caught in the cross fire between your manager and other groups, or are attempting to carry the corporate message down from on high. In any case, the first reaction that you encounter will often be one of great anger or anxiety. Listen! Let your audience know that you are receptive to its concerns.

3. *Don't pass the buck.* It's easy to tell others, "They [my manager, the corporate office] are the bad guys. I don't necessarily believe in what they are doing; I'm just trying to do my job." Don't do it. You will just destroy your credibility in your organization and create a potential problem with your own management. It's more effective to say, "I'm sorry that you are angry and upset about this. I may have not created this situation, but I'm responsible for managing it. I'm willing to do anything within my level of control to address your concerns. What can I do to make things easier for you?"

4. *Start out at point zero.* Don't be surprised if the managers who are confronting you stay focused on the past. They may begin by arguing that the current situation could have been prevented (if only someone in your department had taken appropriate action) or that it represents part of a pattern of intentionally disruptive behavior that's being carried out by other people in your organization. Don't respond to these attacks defensively. At the same time, don't allow others to wallow in the past. Lead with a statement that keeps them "future-focused": "You may be right about all of that. My question to you is, given the situation as it presently stands, what can you and I do at this point to improve the situation?"

5. *Offer to act as a sounding board, but be careful of making promises you can't keep.* Let's assume that you are your company's security manager and have just been told to implement some unpopular changes in security procedures, such as performing personal inspections on all packages and carrying cases coming in or out of your company. In response to a manager's complaint about this policy, you might say "I know this is going to create some problems for you, and I'll be glad to carry your concerns back to our vice president. In the meantime, however, we have to assume that this procedure is going to go into effect on Monday. Why don't we exchange some ideas about any steps that

you and I can take to minimize the problems that this could create for your group?''

• **Seek a level playing field.** It would be nice if all of us started out with the same level of influence and control in our organizations, but that's not quite the way it happens. Cliques form among people who have things in common. At one of my previous employers, a major defense contractor, there was a big distinction between those employees who had previously served in the military and those who lacked military experience. In one of my client companies an exclusive clique of employees who have received advanced degrees from certain prestigious universities has formed.

When faced with these types of interpersonal inequities you have one of three options. You can threaten to take your ball and go home; in other words, you can react in an angry and confrontive way to such cliques whenever you see them in operation. This option only serves to alienate you more from the people whose support and assistance you depend upon for your job survival. The second option is to withdraw from the field by cutting yourself off from others in the clique. A more reasonable option is to seek a level playing field (one in which you aren't at an immediate disadvantage) by looking for ways to work around such cliques. For example, I know of a highly skilled individual who is one of the few women managers in her department. Each week the guys in the department (along with several key senior-level executives) meet together over tennis and golf. She has countered by forming her own internal support network—her company's first executive club for women. As the club's founder and president, she is able to form close working relationships with women managers in other departments, while demonstrating her leadership and organizing skills.

The technique that you select might be quite different. The only requirements for seeking a level playing field are that you look for an interpersonal setting that (1) occurs on a regular basis, (2) removes you and others from your regular work routine, (3) is stimulating and enjoyable, (4) is a situation in which you feel in control (in your element), and (5) is likely to be of interest to other managers and executives in your company.

Strategy 3: Build Consensus

There are two ways to view negotiation sessions with other managers. First, you can view such sessions as win-lose conflicts. The alternative, viewing negotiations as problem-solving sessions, provides the following advantages:

- It helps you remain task-focused and calm, instead of mentally gearing yourself up for battle. As a result, you can usually accomplish more during the session with less stress and fatigue.
- It enables you and the other party to unite your time and energy in working on a common problem. It's a more productive approach, resulting in less waste and loss for both parties. In contrast, with a conflict approach a large part of your available time and energy are spent trying to defeat the other party.
- It leads to enduring and transferrable solutions. In contrast, a conflict approach is usually a superficial and temporary approach to the problem at hand, since it accomplishes nothing more than coercing or forcing the other party to move toward your objective. It doesn't encourage you and the other party to uncover the underlying causes of problems or to move to permanent solutions. In addition, with a conflict approach your goals are secure only as long as you are able to maintain pressure on the other party and as long as all personal relationships are stable. If the other party is replaced by someone else or other people enter the picture, you are back to square one.
- It enables you to accomplish your work objectives while preserving and enhancing your work relationships. A conflict approach usually represents a pyrrhic victory—you may win the battle but lose the war. During tough times you don't need to create additional enemies.

Keep in mind that some conflicts are unavoidable. If you are trying to extradite yourself from a conflict, the Stress Situations Guide in the Tool Kit for Challenge 2 may prove helpful.

A problem-solving approach to negotiation is based on the use of the following tactics:

- **Achieve focus.** A good starting point for negotiation is to achieve focus, that is, to visualize clearly what you and the other party want to take away from, and what you bring to, the negotiation. Before sitting down and talking with the other manager, make brief notes in the following areas:
  - *Purpose.* What issues or relationship problems do you want to resolve?
  - *People.* Are you talking to the right person? Is this manager "in the driver's seat" of the problem? Do other people need to be brought into this discussion? Who are the real stakeholders in this situation?

- *Goals.* What do you hope to accomplish in this meeting? Is your goal realistic, considering your starting point for discussion and the time allotted for the discussion? What do you think the other manager wants to accomplish? What's on his or her agenda? What are the common objectives or stakes—those areas in which you and your partner share the same goals?
- *Assumptions.* People often walk into negotiations with a lot of excess baggage, that is, unfounded assumptions or complaints. What are some of yours? Your partner's?
- *Side issues.* What side issues or personality problems are likely to be brought up that could potentially derail your negotiations? What steps could you take during your initial discussion to help you and your partner keep on track?
- *Trade-offs.* From your point of view, what is and is not negotiable? What are you willing to give up? On what issues are you willing to compromise? What are the potential "stuck" points in your negotiation—those issues over which conflicts are most likely to arise between you and the other party? Do you have any initial suggestions for ways to overcome these stuck points?

Postpone your discussion until you are able to take the time to address these questions. Unless you establish a clear focus for your negotiation, you will find yourself drifting to irrelevant topics or becoming caught up in petty arguments. These questions can help you formulate a solid game plan for approaching your negotiation discussion and for performing preliminary problem solving in advance of this session. Use the Negotiation Planning Form in the Tool Kit to develop an overview of your negotiation plan.

- **Set the stage.** A number of research studies have shown that much of what occurs during the first three minutes of any human interaction sets the stage for the outcome of that interaction. Unfortunately, sometimes when people first enter a negotiation they are so caught up in their own thoughts that they fail to pay attention to the small things that set the stage for a discussion. Here are some examples of things we've all been guilty of:

- Being so preoccupied with unrelated thoughts, that the other person interprets your inattentiveness as disinterest in the discussion
- Being in such a rush to get to the core issues that you bulldoze your way through the discussion, ignoring clues that suggest that the other person is anxious or defensive

- Making insensitive comments that are likely to be viewed by the other person as caustic or critical

To increase your chances for a successful negotiation, take some time to set the stage. Carefully consider the best time and place to hold your discussion. Whenever possible, try to have the discussion well in advance of any critical time limits for decisions that have to be jointly made to prevent the other party from feeling backed against the wall. Look into the possibility of meeting outside your routine work areas, such as a conference room or your company cafeteria (during off-hours). Try to remain relaxed and calm during the first few minutes of the discussion. Thank the other party for agreeing to take the time to meet with you. While it's not necessary to engage in extended small talk, a few friendly personal comments can certainly help make the other person feel more comfortable.

Apart from these suggestions, it's important to consider the best way of introducing the subject at hand. Julian Kaufmann, director of staffing and organizational development for Allied-Signal Corporation, offers the following suggestions as possible door-openers to the discussion: "Use statements such as 'I'm concerned that our groups are not working together as well as they could,' 'I feel that we are missing opportunities to partner together,' 'I want to see if we can rewrite our contract (implicit agreement on how the teams work together) with each other,' 'I'd like to find out if I can be of additional support or service to you.' "[6]

Once you've opened the discussion on a positive note, avoid the tendency to rush in and begin problem solving. Instead, step back and provide a brief overview of how you view the issue and what you hope the two of you will accomplish during the time you have available. Here's a sample overview:

> "As you know, both of our teams are responsible for providing our external customers with information on product installations. I think we'd both have to agree that at times there has been some confusion regarding the respective roles that our teams should play in providing this information and in resolving questions directed by our customers. At times, our customers feel that they are dealing with two or more organizations, rather than one united company. I was hoping that during the next hour you and I could reach some agreement regarding the most effective way that our teams could support each other on this func-

tion. Do you think that's a reasonable goal to set for ourselves?"

Then step back and invite the other person to modify or revise this goal statement as she sees fit. Try to reach agreement on what the two of you hope to accomplish during your time together before moving forward.

• **Seek understanding.** Once you've set the stage for the discussion, the next step is to seek a better understanding of your negotiating partner. This involves the following three steps, which should be accomplished during the first part of your discussion.

1. *Separate interests from positions.* This is a core negotiation tactic suggested by Roger Fisher and William Ury in their book, *Getting to Yes.*[7] They assume that an individual enters into negotiations armed with a position that represents the desired final outcome of the negotiation for that person. Such positions tend to be relatively fixed and narrowly defined. For example, an individual may approach his spouse and say, "I've decided that we should spend this vacation at the Bar-B-Dude Ranch in West Montana." The spouse may counter with, "There's no way that I'm going to waste my time sitting on a horse for two weeks. I want to go visit my mother in Iowa."

As you can see, such positions leave little room for negotiation. They must either be accepted or rejected on a yes or no basis. Interests, on the other hand, are the underlying motives and concerns that drive the position. They tend to be numerous and vary widely in the relative importance that people attach to them. Even if different people do not hold identical positions, they may have the same interests, which can serve as an essential starting point for negotiation.

To get some clarity on this, consider the illustration presented in Figure 6-3. The circle represents all possible options for solving a problem. If each party aims at this target zone with its narrowly defined positions, the parties will have a difficult time locating a common area of agreement.

If, however, they begin with a discussion of interests rather than positions, they will usually find that they can locate some initial area of agreement. In our vacation example, if the husband and wife were to ask each other the magical question "Ideally, what would you like to take away from our vacation? What types of things are most important to you?" they might find that they both want many of the same things (Figure 6-4).

Use the following questions to identify the other party's interests:

Figure 6-3.   The Target Zone.

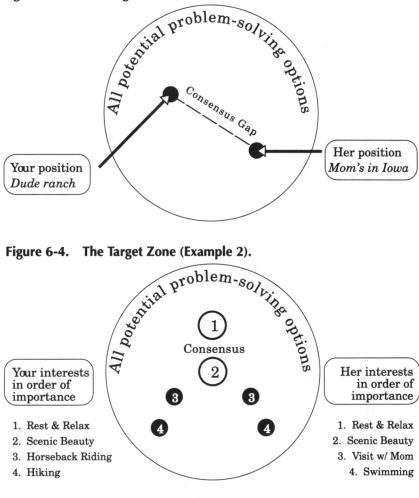

Figure 6-4.   The Target Zone (Example 2).

- What outcomes are most important to you in this situation?
- Ideally, if we can come to an agreement that you are happy with, what types of things would it involve?
- You've mentioned a number of decision factors that are important to you. Which ones are most important?

2. *Understand the other party's underlying fears.* During an organizational negotiation people often operate from a hidden agenda that grows out of their key underlying fears and concerns. At first, few, if any, of these fears and concerns will be laid openly on the table. People are reluctant to expose themselves to additional risk, and they may be

concerned that exposing their fears will cause others to view them as weak and vulnerable. Regardless of their source, many of their fears center around the potential for loss. Here are some of the more common fears that you may encounter:

- *Loss of face*—fear that you will expose problems that make them look bad or will propose a project that they aren't capable of handling
- *Loss of resources*—the limited pie, that is, fear that giving up something to you will translate to a loss (staff, influence, budget) for the other person
- *Loss of control*—fear that a proposed change will mean that some control will be taken out of one's hands
- *Loss of energy*—fear that you are suggesting something that will involve a substantial drain on the other person's time and energy
- *Loss of stability*—fear that you are stirring up a hornet's nest of issues that neither you nor the other person will be able to control
- *Loss of effort*—fear that you are simply blowing smoke and that your proposal will only lead to wasted effort

Think for a minute about the managers with whom you wish to negotiate. What are some of their potential fears? What might they fear losing as a result of your negotiation?

Never attempt to uncover these underlying fears and concerns by approaching the other person head-on in a confrontational fashion. No matter how correct you are, you will only cause him to close up like a clam. Try to probe very carefully, while simultaneously trying to make the other person comfortable enough to disclose her true feelings. For example, you might say, "I'm sure that there are a lot of potential problems with what I've suggested, and it's hard for me to see all of them from my point of view. From where you sit, what are some of the additional concerns that you think we may need to consider?"

3. *Communicate respect for the other party's views.* In my experience, this is one of the simplest and yet most overlooked guidelines in negotiation. In running assessment centers and team-building workshops, I've run into many "listening experts" who frequently sabotage their own negotiation efforts simply by failing to take the time to let the speakers know that they have been heard and that their opinions have been carefully considered. The failure to listen can show up in a variety of behaviors:

- Cutting people off in the middle of sentences
- Immediately countering their ideas without acknowledging that you've heard them
- Remaining poker-faced and providing no verbal or nonverbal reaction
- Frowning, smirking, or giving other nonverbal clues that you've stopped listening before the other party has finished talking
- Responding to a statement with an unrelated comment, showing that you were only partially attending to the other person or that what he said was of little consequence

The simplest and most effective means of conveying understanding is by summarizing what you've heard—restating the key points. If you can't get an affirmative nod from the other person, stay with her until you do, and then move forward.

• **Pursue alignment.** Once a foundation of understanding has been created, your next step is to pursue a line of discussion that aligns you both toward a common win. Begin by summarizing your interests—what's most important for you to take away from the negotiation. At this point, try to refrain from locking into a fixed position or selling a final solution to the problem. Instead, emphasize common wins, those objectives and goals that are common to you and the other party. Whenever possible, reposition your objectives within the context of the other person's needs. As an example, here is the approach that a production manager might take if she wanted to convince a sales manager to allow production personnel to accompany the sales team on customer site visits:

> "Earlier you said that the most important thing from your point of view was getting us to accelerate our response time to new product designs. I agree with you entirely on this, as that's one of the goals I've set for improving my team's performance. That's why I want our people to accompany you on the customer site visits. We estimate that we are encountering a two- to three-day slowdown in getting customer feedback from your group, and we spend even more time going back and forth attempting to accurately interpret that feedback. I believe that if my people could accompany you on those visits, we could increase our response time by as much as three to four days. What do you think?"

Another method for pursuing common alignment is to elicit a common vision. This means encouraging the other party to look beyond the immediate problem to his long-term objectives. An organizational development manager, for example, might use the following approach to convince his company's human resources director to support the creation of an in-house assessment center:

> "On several occasions you've mentioned your long-term goal of playing a stronger role in our company's strategic planning process by developing a succession planning program that would help us identify managers who have strong executive potential. I feel that an in-house assessment center would move you a lot closer to this goal by providing an objective data base for evaluating management potential. Another benefit would be that it would help our executives establish more meaningful development goals for their staff."

To pursue alignment, try following these steps:

1. *Identify areas of misalignment.* An ideal negotiation is one in which you and the other party are in complete agreement on three points: the current situation, your approach, and your goals. However, this ideal situation seldom occurs. Instead, negotiations frequently become stuck whenever you and your negotiating partners move out of alignment on one or more of these points.

The current situation. You and the other party need to agree on how you define the current problems. If you can't reach agreement on the current situation, there is no point in going further, because you will be arguing about apples and oranges. Disagreement at this point can occur because each of you enters the discussion armed with different facts and an incomplete view of the problem or because, although you both have access to the same information, you interpret it in different ways. For example, one of you may feel that the situation:

- Does not represent a signficant problem for one or both parties
- Will improve by itself without the need for further intervention

The goal. This refers to your desired end point or what you hope to accomplish during the negotiation. Disagreements on goals may involve:

- Incompatible interests
- Different completion levels for goals (e.g., one party wants a quick-and-dirty solution while the other wishes to invest the time and effort to develop a more permanent solution)
- Disagreements, usually in the form of hidden agendas, regard-

ing who will derive the benefits or payoffs from the solution (e.g., one party may be concerned about how the success story describing the changes jointly put into affect by your two groups will be presented to senior management)

The approach. Even if the other party shares your views concerning where the two of you are starting and where you need to go, you may still disagree regarding the best approach for getting there. This disagreement can center on:

- Which party should control the change process or who should be involved in the change process
- How fast you should proceed to the goal (one of you may prefer a low-risk approach, while the other is impatient for change)
- The methods each of you would like to use to implement change
- The criteria by which success will be measured

As an example, I was brought into an organization to provide consulting advice regarding the implementation of self-directed work teams (SDWT). The manufacturing, engineering, and human resources managers involved in the discussion had previously reached agreement on the desirability of initiating such teams at their facility and on the benefits they hoped to derive from the use of SDWTs. Their major stuck point, however, was how to move beyond the initial pilot program (the creation of two SDWTs in one area of the plant) to broader implementation. The production manager was a gung-ho type who wanted to install SDWTs in all areas of production, while the human resources manager (a very cautious person) wanted to perform a one-year follow-up on the pilot program before going further. The engineering manager, who took a middle-of-the-road position, argued for the gradual phase-in of additional teams at selected sites. I was brought in because all parties knew that without agreement on their implementation approach, they couldn't progress on the project.

2. *Work from areas of least resistance to those of greatest resistance.* While this sounds like basic common sense, I've seen a number of situations in which an individual, in an effort to close out on the negotiation, immediately tried to tackle the issue of greatest resistance and ran directly into a brick wall. During a negotiation you want to *open a path of agreement.* To do this, start with those areas on which you and the other party have already expressed agreement; then move on to minor points of difficulty. If necessary, temporarily table areas of heavy resistance (write them on the flipchart or make note of them so that the other party knows that you are not attempting to ignore these issues), and come back to them at a later time. Another version of this tech-

nique is to encourage the other party to think beyond the limitations imposed by an obstacle. Example:

Other: Given our budget, there's absolutely no way to proceed with those suggestions.

You: You're right. Lack of money could stop us cold. However, if we were to assume that money was not a problem, how would you feel about the idea then?

3. *Look for ways to realign separate viewpoints.* Resistance usually occurs because the other party disagrees with you about the current situation, your goals, or your proposed approach to the problem. Consider ways for bringing these separate viewpoints into greater alignment. If the disagreement centers around your views of the current situation, for example, you might:

- Suspend further discussion until the two of you have an opportunity to work together to gather additional data on the problem
- Ask an impartial third party to review the situation
- Use process analysis to generate a graphic overview of the problem
- Reduce misunderstandings by defining your terms more carefully
- Conduct a joint review of samples, documentation, past performance records, or other data that can provide a more accurate assessment of the problem

Sometimes it's difficult for you and the other party to reach agreement on the current situation because one of you doesn't trust the other's information. Joe Dunsmore, senior marketing manager for AT&T Paradyne, suggests that, rather than directly challenge the other person's data, a more effective approach is to try to obtain an objective perspective from a third person or outside source that both you and your partner respect.[8] Joe suggests that if someone gives you a project schedule you can't trust, you can:

- Test his input with other people who have expertise in this project area
- Hire an external auditor to audit the project schedule
- Benchmark another company to test the input against competitive measures

If you and the other party disagree on the goals you should pursue, you might try some of the tactics we've mentioned, such as separating positions from interests or encouraging the other person to prioritize his interests.

If you and the other party need to seek greater alignment on your approach, you can:

- Use benchmarking to identify approaches that have been successful with other groups or companies
- Invite a third party, such as a consultant with expertise in the area under review, to help troubleshoot the feasibility of alternative approaches
- Look for solution options that enable you to mix and match elements from each of your proposed approaches

4. *Reframe sources of resistance.* Reframing means placing an issue within a different context to help someone to take a different view of it. For example, assume that you are a salesperson for a sports-car dealership. A potential buyer seems interested in a car but is concerned because he's always owned full-size cars, which he associates with greater safety on the road. In this case, reframing might take the form of repositioning the car as a safe choice because it (1) offers air bags, a built in roll bar, and anti-lock breaks, and (2) provides excellent maneuverability and acceleration, features that improve safety on the highways.

5. *Lower the risk level.* If someone is resisting your proposed solution, it may be because it poses a high risk level for her. Consider these ways to reduce risk:

- Suggest that your solution be tried on a temporary, pilot basis before you decide together whether to pursue it
- Provide stringent methods for tracking and evaluating the success of a solution
- Pursue the solution on a small, incremental basis (for example, begin with a single team or a few individuals)
- Offer to have the suggestion reviewed and/or approved by a third-party who can function as adviser and troubleshooter
- Make the other person an owner in the solution by providing him with greater control over the solution and outcome
- Provide face-saving avenues

This last point is especially important if the other party feels that by accepting your solution, he will be acknowledging that he has not properly handled the problem in the past or that he now requires assistance from your team. Face-saving avenues include:

- Avoiding referencing past performance problems ("I told you so")

- Suggesting that the current problem offers learning and improvement opportunities for both teams
- Providing the other party with several options for co-managing the final solution
- Agreeing that the solution currently in place has served a useful purpose over time but needs to be superseded by another solution to meet changing conditions
- Congratulating the other party for having the insight and courage to recognize the need for change

- **Capture commitment.** Assuming that you can reach alignment on current situation, goals, and approach, you are almost home. The last step, and one that is often overlooked, is to capture commitment—making certain that both parties have translated good intentions and innovative ideas into a solid plan of action. This step is extremely important because without it, each party is likely to walk away from the negotiation without a clear agenda for change.

To nail down both parties' commitment, take these steps:

1. *Make commitments explicit.* The key to capturing commitment is to slow down the discussion and force yourself and the other party to define your commitment in clear, behavioral terms. People often want to skim through this step for any of several reasons. First, by the time that you and the other party reach the commitment phase of negotiations, you both may feel exhausted and drained. In addition, no one likes to be viewed as a nitpicker. After all, if the other party pledges to try to be more responsive to your team, can't you take that at face value? There is also a prevalent assumption that fuzzy phrases such as "being more responsive," "being courteous," "giving additional support," and "following approved procedure" have the same meaning to all people. They don't, and that's the problem. If you don't want to be back at the negotiation table in a week, take the time to define your terms. Finally, without a clear commitment process you can't evaluate the success of whatever changes you and your partner are considering. If you can't define it, measure it, and objectively evaluate it, you can't tell if it works. Consider the following examples:

- "We will try to be more responsive" versus "We will make a commitment to respond to your queries within four hours"
- "We will be more courteous" versus "When your people approach any member of my team with questions, I will make sure that we listen to you without shutting you out and that if we can't address your requests we will clearly explain why"
- "Will share information" versus "Starting next Monday, when-

ever a member of my team visits a customer site, if there is information pertaining to product design problems we will pass on this information to you within twenty-four hours"

2. *Define commitment levels.* One technique that I find useful whenever I'm working with several people in a negotiation is to ask them to rate their level of commitment to a solution on a 1–10 scale, with 10 representing full commitment and 1 representing no commitment. This simple suggestion is particularly useful for drawing out noncommittal individuals and for exposing solutions that, while accepted, receive only halfhearted commitment.

3. *Summarize and reinforce each commitment.* To translate the commitment into action, provide your negotiating partner with written notes describing:

- The actions you agree to take
- When you will start and complete these actions
- Who on your team (or the other party's team) will be involved
- How you will track results

After modeling these steps, ask the other person to provide the same degree of detail on her commitments. Finally, thank her for her commitment and set a time to follow up on the action plan that the two of you have jointly developed.

The Team Contracting Chart in the Tool Kit can help you and your negotiating partner clearly define your agreement and evaluate the success of your negotiation.

TOOL KIT

Relationship Map

A Relationship Map (Figure 6-2) provides a picture of how your team interacts with other groups.

To create a Relationship Map, first draw a circle in the center of a piece of paper to represent your team. In the space surrounding your team, draw circles to represent those other groups on which your team is most interdependent. You should include on your drawing all internal and (if directly served by you) external customers, suppliers, support functions, and any relevant organizational units, such as sister divisions or your corporate office. Groups that exert the greatest influence on your team should be placed closer to your circle, while less important relationships should be placed further away.

Note that in Figure 6-2 a small arrow is placed behind the sales team and facing into "My Team" to indicate that this relationship is expected to grow much stronger over time. Similarly, a small arrow has been placed behind the corporate office and pointing away from the center of the map to indicate that the corporate office is expected to exert less influence over the team in the future.

Draw lines extending from your team to those groups that depend upon you for support. Then draw lines extending from other groups your team depends on for support or assistance to your team. A two-way arrow indicates an interdependent relationship, and a dotted line indicates an emerging relationship.

You can color-code your lines to indicate the quality of each relationship. For example, you might use green lines to indicate strong relationships, yellow lines to indicate relationships that are under stress, and red lines to indicate serious problems.

You now have the framework in place to locate organizational fault lines. Provide brief descriptions of the types of issues that need to be resolved between your team and each group, and draw a connecting line to that group's major line. You could also box the most critical areas.

A very useful team-building exercise is to give members flipchart paper and have them each construct a Relationship Map for your team. As an added option, have each person mark on the map those areas in which he or she represents the team to other groups. Then post all the maps on a wall and ask members to note similarities and differences. For example, members may disagree on:

- The significance they attach to certain problems
- The level of importance they attach to different groups
- How they view changing relationships with other groups
- How they define team relationship problems
- The role each member currently plays (or should play) in managing certain team boundaries
- The approaches they feel need to be taken to strengthen team relationships

Once your team has discussed its Relationship Maps, a consolidated map can be drawn using input from each member. Another option is to use the blank Team Boundaries Planning Sheet in this Tool

Kit to summarize both problem areas with other teams and suggestions for resolving these problems.

Team Contracting Chart

The Team Contracting Chart (Figure 6-5) provides a convenient method for explicitly outlining the agreement that you and your partner have reached during your negotiations. I recommend that this chart be completed during the negotiation process, with a copy provided to each participant. The chart provides information on the following eight categories:

1. *Problems.* What problems or areas of disagreement are we trying to resolve?
2. *Objectives.* What are our objectives? What are we trying to accomplish?
3. *Actions.* What do we agree to do? Specifically, what actions are we willing to take? What are our commitments to each other?
4. *Time frame.* When will we begin these actions? When will we complete them?

Figure 6-5.   The Team Contracting Chart.

Problems	Objectives	Actions	Time Frame
Accountability	Success Criteria	Follow Up	Results

5. *Accountability.* Who within each of our teams will have bottom-line accountability for accomplishing these actions? What additional authority (if any) will we provide them to enable them to take these actions?
6. *Success criteria.* What criteria will we use to evelute the success of our actions? How do we define a successful outcome?
7. *Follow-up.* When and how will we follow up on the results of our agreement? Who will be involved in the follow-up?
8. *Results.* How well did we do on our action plan? To what degree did we keep our commitments? What issues still remain unresolved.

If-Then Decision Chart

The If-Then Decision Chart (Figure 6-6) is designed to help resolve team boundary issues that involve a number of variables. Let's begin by considering a situation in which two managers are having difficulty reaching agreement regarding the role that each team should play in the co-management of a process. This type of problem is usually resolved in one of three ways.

Figure 6-6.   The If-Then Decision Chart.

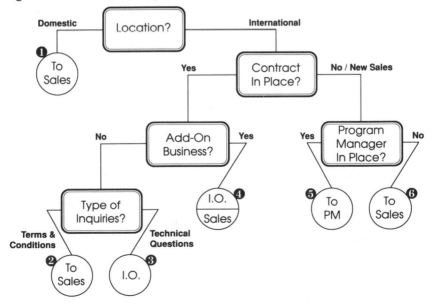

First, one manager may grab control of the process through a unilateral move, such as having the executive management place the process directly under his control. While this approach does help clearly define team responsibilities it also creates additional friction between the affected teams.

Second, the managers can attempt to resolve the problem on a case-by-case basis. This means investing their time in personally negotiating a resolution for every situation that is brought to their attention by their teams. Unfortunately, this provides only a piecemeal approach to the problem and creates an excessive energy drain on both managers.

Third, the managers can decide to share responsibility for managing the process through methods such as standing committees. Again, this is a rather sloppy, time-consuming, and ineffective approach to the problem.

In contrast to these approaches, the If-Then Decision Chart spells out the conditions under which one or another group is to assume responsibility for a particular function. Rather than assign rigid inter-team boundaries, it enables bordering teams to shift their boundaries as needed, to respond to changing conditions.

The chart in Figure 6-6 describes a team negotiation between an international sales team and an international operations (IO) team that was responsible for providing technical support for the sales department in such areas as facilities planning and product installation throughout the world. The following steps were taken to construct the chart.

1. *The teams defined one boundary area for review.* The teams defined their boundary issue in terms of the question "How can we determine the relative role that each team should play in managing relationships with our external customers?"
2. *The teams identified the factors that influenced their boundary decisions.* In this case, five factors were considered:
   - *Customer's location*—was it domestic or international?
   - Was an *existing contract* in place with the customer?
   - If no contract was in place, had a *program manager* already been assigned to develop a proposal for the customer?
   - If a contract was in place, was the customer inquiring about *add-on business* (the purchase of additional products through the existing contract)?
   - If the customer wasn't inquiring about add-on business, what *type of inquiry* was it making (questions concerning the terms

and conditions of the existing contract or technical questions related to the product)?

3. *The teams arranged these factors in their most logical sequence* through the use of a series of interconnecting decision steps (shown in the model). For example, the first question that was chosen was "location of customer," because both teams agreed that for domestic customers, the sales department had the responsibility of working with the customer, so no additional discussion would be necessary.

4. *The teams looked for areas of agreement on boundary management.* Each of the circled areas on the model represent the teams' agreement regarding which team had the responsibility for working with the customer. Once the decision chart had been developed, both teams quickly realized that they agreed on points 1, 2, 3, and 5.

5. *The teams negotiated all stuck points on the chart.* These stuck points were limited to deciding which team had responsibility for point 6 (they finally agreed that sales controlled this area) and point 4 (they agreed to co-manage this area).

The completed chart served as a formal contract between the participating teams, and copies of it were distributed to all team participants.

While it does require some time and effort to construct a chart, the advantage is that it provides a detailed and uniform map for handing difficult boundary decisions. If you decide to use this technique, I suggest that you reach agreement with your negotiating partner to construct a preliminary chart for use on a trial basis over a limited period of time, with the understanding that the two of you will meet at a specified time to revise the chart if necessary.

Team Boundaries Planning Sheet

The Team Boundaries Planning Sheet can help you determine the steps that you and your members can take to manage relationships with other groups more effectively. There are four steps involved in the use of the planning sheet:

This section on team boundaries and its models have been adapted from the text "The PCS Team Development Program; Unit 5: Team Interactions" (Tequesta, Fla.: Parry Consulting Services, 1989). ©1989, all rights reserved.

1. *Identify areas for review.* Identify areas in which you or other members need to improve your representation to other groups or external organizations. Five common types of problems—no representation, poor image mangement, wrong representative, lack of clear guidelines, and ineffective coordination—are described in Figure 6-7. Note that for each problem that has been described by this team, some specific examples have also been provided.
2. *Assess impact.* Determine the relative impact of each problem described in Step 1. Review the "Impact" column in the model.
3. *Develop recommended changes.* Reach agreement with your team regarding ways to improve performance in each problem area. Review the "Recommended Changes" column in the model.
4. *Communicate changes to outside groups.* Because many of the changes recommended by your team will directly affect the other groups with which your team interacts, it's important to clearly explain to those groups the types of changes that your team will be making. For example, your team may decide that rather than have several members interact with a group, all contacts between your team and that group will be routed through a single member. In this situation, your team would need to ask the other group to direct all calls and visits to your selected team representative.

Negotiation Planning Form

The Negotiation Planning Form (Figure 6-8) is a simple form you can use to think through some of the major factors that will affect your negotiations with other managers. The chart can also be used in other negotiation sessions to help you troubleshoot potential stuck points or to identify the most effective negotiating approach to take in a given situation.

There are seven steps involved in completing this form:

1. *Work issue.* Briefly describe the issue that you would like to address in your negotiation. As a general rule of thumb, the more specifically you can define your work issue, the easier it will be to resolve it.
2. *My goal/their goal.* Briefly describe your goal for the meeting,

(Text continued on page 200.)

Figure 6-7. Team Boundaries Planning Sheet.

Types of Problems	Examples	Impact	Recommended Changes
❶ **No Representation:** We currently have no one person dedicated to managing relationships with a key work group.	Someone should be representing our team in the weekly production meetings involving engineering and manufacturing.	We currently have no input on decisions which affect our team that are made in these meetings.	Contact Jack and get his OK to have one of us attend the meetings. Have one of us volunteer to attend on a rotational basis.
❷ **Poor Image Management:** Through our dress, actions, or comments, we are presenting the wrong image to outside work groups.	Some of us are being too abrupt and rude in our phone conversations with internal customers. Instead of just saying, "No, we can't handle that," we need to say, "Let's see how we can help you."	We are beginning to get customer complaints on this, and it's come to the attention of our director.	Review and agree on guidelines for phone conversations. Honestly confront each other when we see violations. Perhaps take a training program on handling difficult customers on the phone.
❸ **Wrong Representative:** We need to select someone else to represent our team to other work groups.	Currently Bill is representing us to the finance department, but he seems to have difficultly interpreting their procedures.	We often have to go back to finance to clarify procedures. This is slowing us down a lot.	We need to select as a financial representative someone who has a stronger background in finance.

(continues)

Figure 6-7. Continued

Types of Problems	Examples	Impact	Recommended Changes
❹ **Lack of Clear Guidelines:** More than one team member represents the team to outside groups, and each team member follows different guidelines when interacting with outside groups.	Some of us have taken a hands-off approach to our vendors, while other team members feel free to provide vendors with a lot of information about our operation.	We could put some vendors in an unfair competitive position by having access to information that other vendors are denied. If this gets out of hand it could also jeopardize our position as a government contractor.	We need to draft written guidelines regarding the types of information to which vendors will have access.
❺ **Ineffective Coordination:** We are not coordinating our separate contacts with external work groups.	Last week three members of our team contacted the technical publications department and pushed to get their own projects out the door. The problem was especially bad because each team member spoke with different people in the publications group.	This creates a bad image with other departments— as if we don't know what we are doing. It also makes it difficult for support groups to determine our priorities.	Once a week, we should meet to clarify our requirements for such areas as the publications group. We could determine our relative priorities for completion times and send each group a written list summarizing our jobs, their relative priorities, and our required completion times.

Figure 6-8. The Negotiating Planning Form.

Work Issue:

My Goal	Their Goal	My Interests		
		Nonnegotiable	Negotiable	
My Assumptions	Their Concerns	How to Address	Common Wins	

that is, what you would ideally like to take away from the negotiating session. In the adjoining space marked "Their Goal," try
to identify the goal of your negotiating partner.

3. *My interests: nonnegotiable/negotiable.* Describe those interests
   that you consider to be nonnegotiable. These are the interests
   that, if not met, would cause you to break off negotiations and
   pursue some other avenue to address your needs. In the "Negotiable" column, list, in relative order of importance, those interests on which you are willing to compromise.

   Now step back and look at these two sections. If you've
   placed everything in the nonnegotiable area, you are entering
   your negotiation with a rigid and inflexible position, and you
   are likely to move quickly to a stalemate with your negotiating
   partner. If you've listed everything in the negotiable area you
   may be giving away the store. Finally, if you aren't able to rank
   order your negotiable interests, you need to more clearly define
   your needs and objectives.

4. *My assumptions.* Describe any assumptions that you have about
   the negotiations. The assumptions that you bring to the negotiation will greatly influence the approach you take during the
   negotiation. For example, if you assume that your negotiating
   partner is under great time pressure to resolve your common
   problem, then you will be more likely to drag your feet during
   the discussion, hoping that the pressure to close out on the negotiation will force the other party to make generous conces-
   sions. In this respect, your assumptions are danger areas that
   need to be kept in check as you move through your negotiation.
   During your discussion, look for clues that can help you determine the validity of your assumptions.

5. *Their concerns.* Describe what you think may be some of the
   major concerns of your negotiating partner. What are they
   afraid of losing (review Strategy 3, Tactic 3)?

6. *How to address.* List suggestions you have regarding any actions
   you could take, or statements you could make, that would help
   address these concerns.

7. *Common wins.* List ways in which achieving a desired outcome
   in the negotiations would generate wins for both you and your
   negotiating partner. Keep these wins in mind, and refer to them
   early in your negotiating session.

Once you've completed the form, try to use the information you've
provided on it to create a good overview of your upcoming negotia-

tion. In addition, you may want to review your completed form with a trusted friend or associate and revise the form on the basis of the new input.

Notes

1. Harold P. Weinstein and Michael S. Liebman, "Corporate Scale Down: What Comes Next?" *HRMagazine* (August 1991), pp. 33–37.
2. Steven Covey, *The 7 Habits of Effective People* (New York: Simon & Schuster, 1989).
3. Interview with Jim Yager, assistant executive director of management services, South Florida Water Management District, May 1993.
4. Interview with Ed Nolan, vice president of human resources, Eckerd Drug Company, May 1993.
5. Interview with Joe Dunsmore, senior marketing manager for AT&T Paradyne, May 1993.
6. Interview with Julian Kaufmann, director of staffing and organizational development for Allied-Signal Corporation, March 1993.
7. Roger Fisher and William Ury, *Getting to Yes: Negotiating Agreement without Giving In* (New York: Penguin Books, 1987).
8. Interview with Joe Dunsmore.

A
Final
Word

Renew and Reenergize Yourself

In the previous chapters I introduced strategies for overcoming some of today's most difficult management challenges. My sincere hope is that you've been able to extract from these strategies some information that can help you become a more effective manager and team leader. I'm sure that you recognize, however, that during turbulent times not only your management skills but also your personal fortitude and motivation are sorely tested. For this reason, in this final chapter, I'm going to focus on seven simple actions you can take to support your professional growth, maintain a high level of personal energy and enthusiasm, and apply the teachings contained in this book to your situation.

Action 1. Avoid Technical Obsolescence

As work environments become increasingly characterized by leaner reporting structures and highly self-directed teams, employers will be unable to afford the luxury of maintaining managerial purists—managers who view themselves within the traditional roles of administrators and directors. Instead, managers will be expected to roll up their sleeves and provide solid technical contributions to their teams. Those managers who are hesitant to take a hands-on approach to their work will find themselves with fewer job opportunities. In tomorrow's workplace, more than ever before, job security will depend on one's willingness to maintain a high level of technical proficiency. A general guideline will be that if you aren't willing to put in the effort needed to keep up with your field, you will need to consider moving into another line of work.

To keep your technical skills finely honed, I suggest the following steps:

1. *Form a clear picture of your technical development needs.* One way to do this is to use the Team Benchmarking Form in Challenge 5 to map out your professional development needs by identifying the new job requirements you anticipate encountering over the next few years and the technical skills that could help you meet these requirements.
2. *Skim your professional organizations' newsletters to keep abreast of off-site workshops that can help you build technical skills.*
3. *Put your technical skills to the test.* Looking back over the past three months, can you name one job or project in which you've been personally involved as a technical contributor that has pushed your technical competence to the limit? Did you invite into the project someone who could provide you with impartial feedback on this project?
4. *Don't be afraid to learn from other people on your team.* Don't fall into the ego trap of assuming that because you're a manager, you have nothing to learn from your staff. In the future, the most successful managers will be those who are wiling to continue to play the role of learner.
5. *Whenever possible, import new talent.* Give yourself and your team a blood transfusion by inviting in guests such as professionals from other companies or university instructors. See if you can obtain for a temporary assignment someone from another group who has the specialized technical skills you would like to graft on to your team.
6. *Identify one person in another organization who has developed a reputation for having exceptional technical skills, and benchmark your professional expertise against this individual.* Make it a point to ask this person about her professional development goals and the steps she is taking to sharpen her technical skills.
7. *As you work to strengthen your skills, give some thought as to the percentage of your skills that are contextual—highly specialized skills that are not easily transferable to other environments.* They may be skills related to knowledge of your company's unique methods and procedures. In difficult times, portable skills provide more job security than do contextual skills.

Action 2. Maintain Literacy of Electronic Information Technology

In the past few months, I've read five different studies on projections for how the workplace is likely to change over the next ten years.

While they differ in many respects, they all have one thing in common. Without question, each study suggests that within ten years we will regard computer literacy much the same as we currently regard print literacy. By computer literacy I mean not only a knowledge of programming but also the ability to understand how new hardware and software systems can be applied to your work and at least a rudimentary familiarity with those systems. To increase your computer literacy, follow these steps:

1. There probably are certain people in your organization who usually are the first to make use of new technology—paging system, portable fax/modem, laptop computer. Make a point to keep up with the new hardware and software systems these people are using and find out about the types of productivity increases they are obtaining from these new tools.
2. Build your computer competence by taking a basic computer course at your local university or by asking a team member to provide you with personal coaching.
3. If you feel uncomfortable with these options, scout around for someone who provides this type of instruction on an individual basis.
4. Scan professional journals for reviews on new software applications that are specific to your field.
5. Stay alert to new software or hardware tools that are being considered for use by your department, and find out as much as you can about these systems well in advance of their introduction.
6. Take out a subscription to one of the journals that specialize in providing reviews and analysis of new software and hardware packages.

Action 3. Conduct Frequent Checkups

Your management style isn't set in cement; it can rapidly change over time. So too can your organization's management requirements and your team's leadership needs. If I asked your senior managers to create a list of things that describe the ideal high-performance manager, that list would be very different from one they would have generated five years ago. I recommend that you conduct frequent checkups to determine how your management style is viewed by others in your organization and to evaluate your performance in terms of the shifting performance expectations of your organization. There are several ways to do this:

1. *Conduct a yearly audit of your management style through one of the many commercially available management feedback surveys or through the use of some of the diagnostic instruments provided in this book.* Ask your in-house organizational development specialist or training manager for advice on how to administer and interpret the survey you choose.
2. *Regularly attend workshops that can help you observe your management style in action.* For example, my company offers a portable communication assessment program that evaluates managerial communication on the dimensions of problem solving, group decision making, time-limited data exchange, and negotiation and presentation skills. Assessment programs can enable you to condense a variety of simulated management experiences into a one-day or two-day time interval and can help you obtain feedback from trained observers, other workshop participants, and self-observations of videotaped exercises.
3. *If you feel that you have established a high trust level with your team, consider conducting a yearly hats-off session, in which you invite members to offer candid suggestions for ways that you can improve your performance as a manager.*
4. *Stay alert to changing employee expectations in your company.* Some organizations conduct yearly employee opinion surveys or corporate culture surveys, which can provide useful clues regarding important shifts in employee attitudes. For example, if survey responses indicate that teams are becoming less trustful of the information and assistance they receive from other departments, this conclusion may have implications for your team's relationships with its internal customers. If no such surveys are used by your organization, examine the NWNL *Workplace Stress Survey* discussed in the Tool Kit in Challenge 2.

Action 4. Stay Alert to Self-Defeating Management Behavior

During tough times, there are five management behaviors that are especially damaging to team performance. Keep alert to situations that may indicate that these behaviors are becoming part of your management style:

1. *Poor decision making.* Failure to balance risk taking (shooting from the hip without recourse to adequate information) and time urgency (waiting too long to finalize decisions).
2. *Inability to form influential networks.* Becoming a 'solo fighter'

and trying to win all your battles by yourself without first building an adequate base of influence.
3. *Becoming closed off and uncommunicative.* Becoming less open and receptive to feedback from your managers, peers, and team.
4. *Inflexibility.* Being unable to adapt to new methods, priorities, or organizational direction. Holding on to the past at all costs.
5. *Micromanagement.* Confusing decisive leadership with micromanagement and attempting to deal with confusion and uncertainty by overmanaging the day-to-day functions of your team.

Action 5. Avoid the Mushroom Cellar

If there's one theme that I have continually emphasized in this book it's that during difficult times it's essential to examine your function and skills within the larger context of the changes occurring in your department, organization, and professional field. To keep abreast of such changes, take the following steps:

1. *Have weekly luncheon meetings with professionals from other departments or organizations who have gained reputations for being on the cutting edge of your field.* If you haven't developed a strong professional network, I recommend that you read Strategy 7: Secure Lifelines in my book, *Lifeboat Strategies.*
2. *Attend professional meetings, and keep up with your reading in professional journals.* A time-effective way to do this is to pencil in one day per month on your calendar when you can go to your public library to conduct a quick skim of the table of contents of leading magazines or use your library's electronic menu to zero in on relevant articles by subject area.
3. *If you don't have the time to keep up personally, use surrogates.* See if your team members would be willing to attend local professional meetings on a rotational basis and keep you alert to special speakers or events directly related to your career goals. In the same way, assign each team member the job of tracking a different technical or business journal and circulating for reading any articles pertaining to important trends or technical advances in your field.
4. *If you haven't done so, read "Challenge 1: Develop a Fast Draw" in this book for information about how to keep track of large-scale organizational changes.*
5. *Maintain solid relationships.* One of the best ways to keep abreast

of new developments is to be the kind of person with whom others feel free to share new information and ideas without fear of criticism or censure.

Action 6: Periodically Stop and Regroup

Both the great advantage and the great disadvantage of attempting to manage in a turbulent business environment is that you must face choices you otherwise wouldn't have had to deal with. During times of rapid organizational change it's not unusual to discover that groups are suddenly recombined, job responsibilities shifted, priorities reshuffled, and the demands on teams sharply escalated. Amid these changes it's important for you to be able to stop periodically and regroup—to reevaluate your personal career goals and your team's core mission. The following steps can help you make timely midcourse corrections to your professional career:

1. *Reassess your goals and priorities on a regular basis.* Every few months, make it a point to arrive at work a few minutes early, sit down at your desk before the phones begin to ring, and ask yourself the following questions:

"At this point in time how do I define career success?"

"What do I want out of my job? Has this changed a lot since last year?"

"Where has my team been directing most of its efforts during the last few months? What's been the payoff for this? At this point in time, do we need to consider redirecting our time and energy?"

"Of all of the problems on my plate, which one could potentially give me the most heartburn? What have we been doing so far to deal with this problem? What decisive action could we take that would make a significant dent in it?"

"What opportunities are emerging from the changes we are now experiencing? How can we best capitalize on these opportunities?"

"What's working well for our team? How would I define our current strengths as a team?"

"How do we need to strengthen ourselves? When I form a vivid picture of how I'd like to see my team performing a year from now, what comes to mind? How does this picture compare with my team's current performance? What can I do as a manager to support these changes?"

2. *Once a quarter, meet with your team to compare notes on how you and your members view your team's strengths and development needs.*

3. *On a regular basis, evaluate the desirability and feasibility of your work and career goals.* Do they still meet your needs, and, given current conditions, are they still achievable or do they need to be changed? If you have some uncertainty regarding the best way to define these goals, you may find it helpful to read "Strategy 6: Chart Your Own Course" in my book *Lifeboat Strategies*.

Action 7: Put It to Work

While there's no secret recipe for managing in tough times, I hope this book has provided some useful suggestions and guidelines for managing your own situation. The key to developing as a manager is to aggressively look for ways to put new ideas to work. The following honesty quiz can help you determine if you've taken steps to obtain the best possible use from this book.

Honesty Quiz

1. Have you been an active reader? Have you made notes in this book or highlighted key passages?
2. Were you able to identify, from the Survival Quiz, the single greatest challenge now facing your team?
3. As you read this book, did you formulate clear performance improvement goals for your team?
4. Have you completed any of the exercises or assessment materials provided in the Tool Kits?
5. Have you been able to identify at least five new ideas that you can apply to your situation?
6. Have you bounced any of these ideas off your associates? If you haven't done so, remember that one of the best ways of moving yourself to action is to engage the services of a useful troubleshooter.
7. Can you honestly say that you've tried to push yourself out of your own comfort zone by applying new management approaches or setting tough performance goals for yourself? If you haven't as yet done so, identify one stretch goal that you could set for yourself that would support your professional development.

The next few years are likely to provide some of the most difficult and challenging work experiences that American managers have ever encountered. Your savvy as a professional and as a manager will be tested again and again. While it's almost impossible to predict the shape that these challenges might take, I firmly believe that if you apply the strategies, tactics, and tools introduced in this book and remain open and receptive to new ideas, you will maintain your momentum—regardless of the type of minefield you are forced to cross.

Good luck!

Appendix:
Trainer's Guide

As a management consultant and former corporate training manager, I know that often, in the course of reading a book like this one, a reader wishes that there were some easy way to use the book as a training tool. This Trainer's Guide has been designed for that purpose, one of the first times that such a tool has been included in a management book. You will find this section helpful if you are a trainer, management consultant, quality improvement facilitator, human resources specialist, or middle manager who would like to help others learn the strategies, tactics, and tools outlined in this book.

The Guide discusses how to use this book as a resource for conducting four different training workshops: change management, continuous improvement/customer satisfaction, employee empowerment, and team building. Although there are potential applications in the areas of stress management, productivity improvement, leadership development, and time-based competition, as well, I believe that, after reviewing the four workshops I've created, you will be able to construct these additional applications on your own.

Although this book was written primarily for managers, the four workshops can be used with both managers and nonmanagerial professionals. For each workshop, a breakdown of the purpose, learning objectives, recommended participants, required materials, preworkshop assignments, and course times and format is provided. Experienced workshop facilitators will quickly note that these course designs provide only a skeletal framework; each workshop will need to be tailored to the unique requirements of your organization. If your company is already providing training in one of these four subject areas, you may find it useful to incorporate some of the exercises and material contained in these outlines into your existing workshops.

If you have a serious interest in applying this book as a training tool to your organization, please feel free to contact me through my publisher. I would be happy to provide additional suggestions for helping you extract greater value from these workshops.

CHANGE MANAGEMENT

Purpose

This workshop shows participants how to anticipate and successfully adapt to changes that can affect their team's performance. During the workshop, participants learn how to scan their organization for impending changes, plan ahead to prepare to meet these changes, and evaluate their personal effectiveness for coping with change.

Time Required

3 hours 45 minutes

Learning Objectives

As a result of attending this workshop participants will:

1. Map out large-scale organizational changes that will have a significant impact on their team's performance
2. Develop a plan for preparing their team to manage these changes effectively
3. Set up a team early-warning system for tracking these changes
4. Look for ways to increase their personal adaptability to change

Participants

The ideal size is twenty participants, with at least two people present from each participating department or major function.

Materials Required

Prior to the workshop, assemble the following materials:

1. Flipchart pad and easel
2. Assorted color markers

3. Masking tape or pushpins
4. One copy of *Crossing the Minefield* for each participant

Before the Workshop

Approximately two weeks prior to the workshop, provide participants with a copy of *Crossing the Minefield* and ask them to read:

- Welcome to Oz (also, complete the Job Survival Quiz)
- Challenge 1: Develop a Fast Draw

Ask participants to be prepared to discuss the following questions in class:

- What types of large-scale organizational and business changes are occurring now that could directly affect the performance of your unit (division or department) and team?
- Based on what you've read, what are some key steps that teams can take to increase their readiness to respond to large-scale changes?

Workshop Content

Part I: Introduction (30 minutes)

1. Goals (15 minutes)
Introduce the program and discuss workshop goals and learning objectives.

2. Change Management (15 minutes)
Ask participants to discuss what comes to mind when they think of the term *change management*. Discuss the differences and similarities in their views, and then offer the following definition for use in the workshop:

> Change management is the process through which we seek to anticipate large-scale organizational and environmental changes, and successfully adapt our performance to meet these changes.

Part II: Importance of Change Management (15 minutes)

1. Review Organizational Examples (15 minutes)

Suggest to participants that the best way to understand the importance of this workshop is to share some examples of successful and unsuccessful organizational attempts to adapt to change. Ask participants to share examples of:

- Companies that have been able to enter new markets or introduce new technologies by quickly capitalizing on major changes
- Companies that have lost markets or become unprofitable by failing to keep pace with critical changes in their customers, technologies, or business environments

Part III: Learning How to Anticipate Change (1 hour 15 minutes)

1. Crystal Ball Exercise (Challenge 4) (30 minutes)

Have participants complete the exercise as a means of identifying emerging organizational changes that are likely to significantly affect the performance of their departments and teams.

2. Change Analysis Chart (Challenge 1) (45 minutes)

Explain that in order to capitalize on change, teams need to be able to clearly determine how these changes are likely to affect their performance. Ask participants to join with others from their teams to form groups of two to four people and to select for discussion one of the changes identified in the Crystal Ball Exercise. Provide a brief overview of the Change Analysis Chart. Give participants twenty minutes to analyze their selected change through the use of this chart; then ask them to take an additional fifteen minutes to list four to five steps that their teams could take during the next month to begin to prepare for this change.

Part IV: Early-Warning Systems (60 minutes)

1. Introduce the concept (10 minutes)

Remind participants that another important change management factor involves the ability of team members to create early-warning systems (EWS) for keeping one another informed of changes on a timely basis. Ask participants to identify, from their preworkshop readings, some of the major conditions of effective EWS.

2. Design an early-warning system (50 minutes)

Challenge each team to use the next thirty minutes to describe on a flipchart one EWS that would serve the team's needs. At the same time, invite the teams to skim Challenge 1 to glean ideas for use in this exercise. Finally, take an additional twenty minutes to have two teams review the EWS they've created and invite other participants to offer suggestions on how the plans could be improved.

Part V: Increasing Your Adaptability to Change (45 minutes)

1. Job Survival Quiz (5 minutes)

Give participants five minutes to review their scores from the Job Survival Quiz and to determine which of the four categories (resistive, retrospective, reactive, or preemptive) best describes the approach that they take to cope with change.

2. Change Management Model (10 minutes)

Explain that a key factor in determining a team's ability to meet new changes successfully is the degree to which members are able to adapt to change. On the flipchart draw a copy of the Change Management Model and briefly review the chart's two dimensions (focus of time/focus of control) and four categories as a model for personal adaptivity.

3. Personal Adaptability Audit (30 minutes)

Suggest that it's possible for individuals to exhibit some characteristics from each of the four change management categories. For example, someone may be largely preemptive but may have difficulty making midcourse corrections in his plans in response to new information. To the degree that people can honestly inventory their personal behavioral strengths and weaknesses, they stand a better chance of becoming effective managers of change. Explain that the final workshop exercise will involve such a personal adaptability audit.

Ask participants to reflect on a recent change that they would like to have handled more effectively. If they have difficulty recalling such an experience, have them identify an impending change that they feel may be difficult to manage. Give participants ten minutes to identify, from the results of their Job Survival Quiz or from their experiences, those behaviors that serve as personal strengths for helping them to meet new changes successfully. At the same time, ask them to identify one or two behaviors that may be keeping them from being even more successful and one action that they could take during the next two weeks to begin to change these behaviors.

For example, if an individual's improvement area involves procrastinating on responding to change, that person's improvement plan might involve:

- Setting up a clear time line to serve as a reminder of when to take action
- Breaking down large-scale changes into smaller, bite-size steps
- Teaming up with a partner who can point out situations in which the person procrastinates
- Keeping handy a list of the problems that are likely to be created if timely action is not taken

Next, ask each person to select a partner (preferably someone who works with or knows him well) and take ten minutes to review the results of this personal adaptability audit with the partner (twenty minutes for each pair) and to invite the partner's feedback and suggestions.

Part VI: Program Summary (10 minutes)

Summarize the goals and objectives of the program, and express your hope that participants have been able to extract valuable information from the workshop. Address final questions from participants, and close.

CONTINUOUS IMPROVEMENT/CUSTOMER SATISFACTION

Purpose

This workshop is designed to help members contribute more effectively to their organizations' continuous improvement programs and to understand the steps they can take to support increased customer satisfaction. During the workshop, participants learn how to identify improvement opportunities, link improvement efforts to customer requirements, and initiate improvement projects.

Time Required

5.0 hours

Learning Objectives

As a result of attending this workshop, participants will:

1. Develop a better understanding of what continuous improvement is and how it can lead to improved performance.

2. Learn to identify organizational changes that are generating the need for continuous improvement.
3. Discover the steps they can take to foster continuous improvement in their organizations.
4. Explore areas for improvement within their functions.

Participants

The ideal population size is twenty participants, with at least two participants from each participating group, to enable participants to work in pairs. In addition, if at all possible, each participant should have in attendance at least one other person who represents one of the participant's internal customers or suppliers.

Materials Required

Prior to the workshop, assemble the following materials:

1. Flipchart pad and easel
2. Assorted color markers
3. Masking tape or pushpins
4. One copy of *Crossing the Minefield* for each participant

Before the Workshop

Approximately two weeks prior to the workshop, provide participants with a copy of *Crossing the Minefield* and ask them to read Challenge 3: Focus Efforts.

Ask participants to be prepared to discuss the following questions in class:

- What does *continuous improvement* mean to you?
- What changes are now taking place in this organization that might make continuous improvement critical to our success?
- On the basis of what you've read in Challenge 3, how would you describe the relationship that exists between continuous improvement and customer satisfaction?

Workshop Content

Part I: Introduction (30 minutes)

1. Goals (15 minutes)
Introduce the program and discuss workshop goals and learning objectives.

2. Continuous Improvement (15 minutes)
Ask participants what comes to mind when they think of the term *continuous improvement*. Discuss the differences and similarities in these views, and then offer the following definition for use in the workshop:

> Continuous improvement is the process by which we seek to make ongoing improvements in each area of our work, through both large-scale changes and small, incremental improvements.

Part II: Importance of Continuous Improvement (60 minutes)

1. Crystal Ball Exercise (Challenge 4) (60 minutes)
Have participants complete the exercise as a means of identifying recent organizational changes that have made continuous improvement more important to their teams' success.

For example, if participants listed as one of their changes "we are shifting from a cost-plus to a fixed-price contract base, in which we will be forced to 'eat' additional costs above those explicitly stated in our contract," suggest that this change means that quality costs and work inefficiencies will no longer be able to be passed on to the customer and that in the future such problems will have an even greater adverse impact on organizational performance.

Part III: Linking CI to Customer Satisfaction (2 hours 15 minutes)

1. Discussion (15 minutes)
Ask participants: "On the basis of your readings, what implications can we draw about the relationships between customer satisfaction and continuous improvement?" Record participants' ideas on the flipchart and later add the following ideas:

- If quality means meeting customer expectations, then the first step for ensuring the success of any continuous improvement effort involves clearly defining customers' requirements.

- Performance myopia—the inability to see through the eyes of our customers—leads to poor performance and weakened relationships with our customers.
- Because we can't assume that we know what our internal and external customers want and expect from us, it's important that we continuously check our assumptions against hard data.

2. The Performance Map (Challenge 3) (60 minutes)

Review the instructions for completing the map. Ask participants to form groups of two to six people with others from their teams. Using flipchart paper, have each team take thirty minutes to construct a Performance Map laying out up to three outputs that they provide for one internal or external customer. Use the next twenty minutes to have each group solicit feedback from other participants on its maps. It's especially important for teams to obtain feedback from their customers if they are present. Challenge each team to identify from its maps its single most important performance improvement opportunity.

3. Customer Interview Guidelines (Challenge 3) (60 minutes)

Explain that as they use the Performance Map, participants may find that they lack important information on their customers' needs and requirements. Have each team select those individuals in the room who represent one of their internal customers or suppliers. Continue going around the room, recording these customer/supplier matches on your flipchart, until each group has been paired with another group. Next, ask supplier teams to spend the next twenty minutes interviewing their customers on the basis of the Customer Interview Guidelines. At the end of the exercise, take fifteen minutes to solicit from each group one new piece of information that it has obtained from this exercise.

Part IV: Selecting an Improvement Project (60 minutes)

1. Improvement Options Map (Challenge 3) (30 minutes)

Continue to have participants stay in their small groups while they take fifteen minutes to brainstorm as many options as they can for improving the areas they just identified. Next, ask each team to draw on another flipchart paper a copy of the Improvement Options Map. Give the teams twenty minutes to chart all their improvement options on this map and to select from these options those that could serve as the best starting point for improvement (improvement options that are categorized as "sprints" on the map).

2. Project Planning Worksheet (Challenge 3) (30 minutes)

Suggest to participants that one of the best tactics for making improvements is to plan ahead to identify ways to overcome obstacles to improvement projects. Ask participants to select from the options they've charted on their improvement map one that would require a number of actions over several weeks or months. Briefly review with participants the Project Planning Worksheet; then divide them into their teams and give them twenty minutes to outline a potential improvement project based on the improvement option that they've selected.

Explain that lacking solid data on the improvement area under review, participants will be able to provide only a sketchy outline. Participants should try to identify the most important stakeholders and obstacles for each stage of the project, along with suggestions for overcoming these obstacles. At the end of the exercise take twenty minutes to have one team summarize its improvement project to the class, and allow other participants to serve as troubleshooters for this project.

Part V: Program Summary (10 minutes)

Summarize the goals and objectives of the program, and express your hope that participants have been able to extract valuable information from the workshop. Address final questions from participants, and close.

EMPLOYEE EMPOWERMENT

Purpose

This workshop is designed to help members make a stronger contribution to organizational performance through the process of employee empowerment. During the workshop, team leaders learn how to empower fully and to energize team performance. At the same time, team members discover how to become more accountable for performance results and be better prepared to take on broader responsibilities.

Time Required

5 hours 30 minutes

Learning Objectives

As a result of attending this workshop, participants will:

1. Develop a better understanding of what employee empowerment is and how it can lead to improved performance.

2. Learn to identify organizational changes that are generating the need for employee empowerment.
3. Discover the steps they can take to foster employee empowerment within their teams.

Participants

For greatest effectiveness, managers or team leaders should attend this workshop along with their team members. In this way, the team's classroom experiences can serve as a model for transferring the empowerment process to the work site. An ideal population size for this workshop is twenty participants drawn from one or two teams.

Materials Required

Prior to the workshop, assemble the following materials:

1. Flipchart pad and easel
2. Assorted color markers
3. Masking tape or pushpins
4. Two cards per participant
5. One copy of *Crossing the Minefield* for each participant

Before the Workshop

Approximately two weeks prior to the workshop, provide participants with a copy of *Crossing the Minefield* and ask them to read:

- Welcome to Oz
- Challenge 1: Develop a Fast Draw (Strategy 3: Tighten Communication Links)
- Challenge 4: Inspire the Troops (Strategy 2: Challenge the Limits)
- Challenge 5: The Team Benchmarking Chart

Ask participants to be prepared to discuss the following questions in class:

- What does *employee empowerment* mean to you?
- What changes are now taking place in this organization that

might make employee empowerment critical to our success?
- What does it mean for a person to be self-empowered? How does this idea relate to the change management model introduced in the beginning of this book?
- On the basis of your preworkshop readings, what suggestions can you make regarding ways your team can encourage members to become fully empowered?

Workshop Content

Part I: Introduction (30 minutes)

1. Goals (15 minutes)
Introduce the program and discuss workshop goals and learning objectives.

2. Employee Empowerment (15 minutes)
Ask participants what comes to mind when they think of the term *employee empowerment*. Discuss the differences and similarities in their views, and then offer the following definition for use in the workshop:

> Employee empowerment is the process by which individuals become more productive and gain greater job satisfaction by obtaining the skills, authority, and control they need to excel in their day-to-day operations.

Part II: Importance of Employee Involvement (60 minutes)

1. Crystal Ball Exercise (Challenge 4) (60 minutes)
Have participants complete the exercise as a means of identifying recent organizational changes that have made employee empowerment more important to their teams' success.

For example, if participants listed as one of their changes "our customers are demanding a faster response time from us," suggest that faster response times require members to be able to respond to customers directly without going through multiple review and approval levels (thus involving greater empowerment).

Part III: Removing Roadblocks to Empowerment (60 minutes)

1. Empowerment/Enablement (Challenge 4) (5 minutes)
Draw on the flipchart the two-dimensional empowerment model

in Figure 4-6. Briefly summarize the two dimensions (empowerment/ enablement) for participants.

2. Empowerment Profile (25 minutes)

Have participants complete and record their individual profile results on the flipchart (or provide their input anonymously on cards) for joint review. High-scoring statements indicate empowerment strengths; low-scoring statements indicate roadblocks to empowerment. Statements for which wide variations in scores have been found indicate areas in which members are expressing widely different concerns.

3. Empowerment Questionnaire (Challenge 1) (30 minutes)

Using the team's Empowerment Profile as a starting point for discussion, have participants discuss questions 1 through 5 of the questionnaire to pinpoint roadblocks to team empowerment and questions 6 through 8 to identify solutions for overcoming these roadblocks. Have participants select from their list of suggestions one or two ideas for implementation on a trial basis during the next few weeks.

Part IV: The Leader's Role in the Empowerment Process (30 minutes)

1. Communications Assessment Survey (Challenge 1) (30 minutes)

This exercise provides team leaders with a better understanding of how their communication styles set the stage for employee empowerment. Begin by asking participants to provide their views regarding how the four survey dimensions (trust/openness/responsiveness/accessibility) relate to employee empowerment. Then have participants use cards to provide anonymous feedback to their leaders on the twelve survey statements. Ask leaders to review this information privately and later to share with their teams one improvement area that they've identified from this feedback.

Part V: Building Team Bench Strength (60 minutes)

1. The Team Benchmarking Chart (Challenge 5) (60 minutes)

Going back to the two-dimensional empowerment model you had drawn earlier on the flipchart, remind participants that empowering actions are only one dimension of the empowerment process; the other dimension involves actions that prepare members to take over greater responsibilities by building skills and competencies. Explain that the

Team Benchmarking Chart is one of the most effective methods for building team competencies and that during the next hour participants will attempt to apply this chart to their teams.

When completing the chart, participants should include under the "Emerging Responsibilities" column of their chart emerging job responsibilities and those current functions on which they would like to increase their current skill levels. In addition to having teams rate their overall competence level on each job responsibility, ask each member to place a check next to those skills on which she would like additional training or development. This additional step will help teams form a clearer picture of their members' different development needs.

Part VI: Developing Self-Empowerment (90 minutes)

1. Introduce the Concept of Self-Empowerment (20 minutes)

Explain that during the first part of class participants looked for ways to set the stage for empowerment and to remove roadblocks to empowerment. The flip side of this process involves actions that each individual can take to empower himself.

Write on the flipchart this question: "How do people lessen their own personal power?" List participants' responses and then add these if they have not been offered by participants:

- Self-doubt; convincing yourself that you are helpless
- Refusing to take risks
- Not learning/expanding skills
- Defining your responsibilities narrowly
- Offering excuses and blame in place of action
- Focusing your attention on uncontrollables instead of on improvement steps that you can take
- Using the language of failure (Challenge 4)
- Setting safe, unchallenging goals for yourself

2. Problem Scenario (Challenge 1) (60 minutes)

Refer participants to the two-dimensional Change Management Model found in the beginning of the book. Suggest to them that true job survivors are self-empowered; they concentrate on actions that are within their focus of control and they remain future-focused, rather than being locked in the past.

Take forty-five minutes to complete the Problem Scenario Exercise. For each problem card selected, ask members to explain how the problem scenario would test an individual's skills and fortitude.

Suggest to the class that everyone occasionally exhibits certain attitudes and behaviors that get in the way of self-empowerment. Give members ten minutes to privately identify as part of their personal action plan one behavioral change that would move them closer to self-empowerment.

Take five minutes to ask a few volunteers to share their action plans with the class. If appropriate, add additional helpful suggestions.

Part VII. Program Summary (10 minutes)

Summarize the goals and objectives of the program, and express your hope that participants were able to extract valuable information from the program. Address final questions from participants, and close.

TEAM BUILDING

Purpose

This workshop is designed to help participants develop key skills for building effective relationships with other groups.

Time Required

6 hours 45 minutes

Learning Objectives

As a result of attending this workshop, participants will:

1. Understand the importance of building strong supportive relationships with other groups.
2. Discover how their team's performance is viewed by other groups.
3. Have an opportunity to test out, within the workshop, options for strengthening relationships with other teams.
4. Determine the individual role they play as team representatives to other groups.

Participants

The ideal training group consists of team members and leaders from two teams, one of which is an internal customer or supplier to the other.

Materials Required

Prior to the workshop, assemble the following materials:

1. Flipchart pad and easel
2. Assorted color markers
3. Masking tape or pushpins
4. One copy of *Crossing the Minefield* for each participant

Before the Workshop

Approximately two weeks prior to the workshop, provide participants with a copy of *Crossing the Minefield* and ask them to read:

- Challenge 6: Forge Alliances

Ask participants to be prepared to discuss the following questions in class:

- Why, when your organization is experiencing difficult times, is it especially important to forge strong alliances?
- Which of the principles behind positive politics does your team exhibit? Which of these principles does your team expect other groups to follow?
- What types of organizational changes are currently taking place that are making it difficult for groups in your company to maintain good relationships?

Workshop Content

Part I: Introduction (30 minutes)

1. Goals (15 minutes)
Introduce the program and discuss workshop goals and learning objectives.

2. Team Building (15 minutes)

Ask participants what comes to mind when they think of the term *team building*. Discuss the differences and similarities in their views, and then offer the following definition for use in the workshop. Explain that this definition applies specifically to *cross-functional team building*—team building designed to span the boundary lines separating different units:

> Team building is the process by which we seek to build strong relationships with other groups through a better understanding of the steps groups can take to support each other's performance and meet each other's requirements.

Part II: Importance of Team Building (40 minutes)

1. Crystal Ball Exercise (Challenge 4) (30 minutes)

Have participants complete the exercise as a means of identifying emerging organizational changes that are making it difficult for teams to maintain supportive relationships. Examples might include:

- Competition with other teams for limited resources
- A dramatic increase in performance pressure on all teams (increasing the tendency for teams to draw off fire through finger pointing or blame casting)
- Reexamination of the relative roles teams play in meeting organizational goals as the organization puts new procedures and methods into place

2. Importance of Allies (10 minutes)

Post on the flipchart the words "importance of allies." Solicit response to the following question: "On the basis of your experiences and what you've read in Challenge 7, what are some of the reasons it's important for us to overcome these roadblocks and forge alliances with other groups?"

Part III: Managing Team Boundary Lines (3 hours 35 minutes)

1. Team Boundaries (15 minutes)

Ask participants to define, on the basis of their readings, what is meant by the term *team boundaries*. Ask representatives from each team to identify some of the most sensitive issues relating to the boundary lines between their respective teams. Examples might be:

- Disagreements over the roles each team should play in dealing with outside customers or suppliers

- Disagreements over the degree to which requirements are being met
- Confusion about methods used by both teams
- Team objectives that work against each other (e.g., efforts of a credit department to establish extremely conservative criteria for loan approvals that conflict with efforts of the sales department to relax these criteria in order to generate greater sales)

On the flipchart, record in one color all the problems identified by one team and in another color all the problems named by the other team. At the end of the discussion, see if the teams can reach agreement on one issue for review. Circle this issue for later reference.

2. Performance Map (Challenge 3) (2 hour 10 minutes)

Take ten minutes to review the purpose of the map. Explain that the first step in building strong interteam relationships is to understand how each team views the other's performance. Review with participants the instructions for how to complete the *Performance Map.*

Mapping the key outputs will take fifty minutes. Ask the customer team—the team that receives outputs from the supplier team—to identify up to three outputs that it receives from the supplier; then have the supplier team help define these outputs. As soon as the two teams have jointly defined the outputs, write these definitions on the flipchart.

Using two sheets of flipchart paper, take twenty minutes to have the customer and supplier teams separately construct Performance Maps showing how they view the supplier's performance on these outputs. Post the two completed flipcharts for simultaneous viewing, and take an additional twenty minutes to have a representative from each team briefly summarize his team's map and identify similarities and differences between the maps. Whenever the teams appear to disagree on how they view outputs, use the Customer Interview Guidelines in Challenge 3 to determine the reasons for these disagreements.

To map requirements and identify customer needs, you'll use fifty minutes. Challenge the two teams to select, from the three outputs, one output for additional review. Ask the customer team to define its three or four most important requirements for this output, and invite additional clarification from the supplier team on them. Don't proceed until both teams have reached a clear agreement regarding these requirements. During the next twenty minutes, have the two teams create two additional Performance Maps, showing how each team views the supplier's performance on these requirements for the selected output. Following this step, take twenty minutes to have the teams review the two maps and reach agreement on the one requirement in greatest need of improvement.

During the next fifteen minutes, ask the supplier team to identify any actions that the customer team could take to make it easier for the supplier team to meet these requirements. For example, a manufacturing group might ask a design group to take the time to neatly draw and diagram their designs so that there is less chance of a misinterpretation.

3. Create a Team Contract (Challenge 6) (1 hour 10 minutes)

Take ten minues to review the Team Contracting Chart. Explain that at this stage of the workshop each team will be asked to identify steps that it can take to resolve problems with its partner. Ask participants to turn to the Team Contracting Chart. Briefly review the various headings in this chart, and once again divide participants into their respective teams.

Have each team, working separately, take fifteen minutes to summarize on the blank charts the *problem* that it would like to resolve with its partner, its *objectives* for the contracting discussion, and any preliminary *actions* that it would be willing to take to resolve the problem.

Bring the teams together. Beginning with the customer team, ask each team to take five minutes to review its summaries of problems, objectives, and proposed actions. During the next fifteen minutes, have the leaders summarize the actions on which they feel they can agree, and set up a time for the subsequent review of unresolved issues. It is unlikely that all issues will be resolved in this one session. Finally, ask the teams to take twenty minutes to outline on their blank charts the details of their joint contract.

Part IV: Develop Team Guidelines for Managing Boundaries (1 hour 45 minutes)

1. Introduce the Concept (10 minutes)

Explain that teams frequently encounter problems because their members lack a common set of guidelines to follow when representing their team to other groups. To illustrate this point, briefly review the five examples of problems shown on the sample Team Boundaries Planning Sheet (Figure 6–7).

2. Team Boundary Planning Sheet (Challenge 6) (1 hour 35 minutes)

Divide participants into their respective teams, and give each team forty minutes to complete as thoroughly as possible a blank planning sheet. Have the members of each team take fifteen minutes to individually sketch out their responses for the first three columns of the chart (Types of Problems, Examples, Impact). Request that they leave the Recommended Changes column blank until their team has an opportunity to discuss that section.

During the next ten minutes have each team select from its members' lists of problems one problem for team review. Ask each team to select a facilitator to guide the rest of the discussion. The two team facilitators should:

- Summarize the problem on the top of the flipchart
- Take ten minutes to help their respective teams identify representative examples of the problem and determine how the problem is impacting on their performance
- Take twenty minutes to offer potential ideas for resolving the problem and reaching agreement on no more than four ideas for implementation over the next six weeks

Part V: Program Summary (10 minutes)

Summarize the goals and objectives of the program, and express your hope that participants have been able to extract valuable information from the workshop. Address final questions from participants, and close.

Index